Levee

Fall 2019 — Issue 03

Founded in 2018 by Samantha Daniels and Eric Orosco

STAFF

Editorial Director
Samantha Daniels

Creative Director
Eric Orosco

For Betsy Harper,

"Maybe just writing this, just knowing that I feel this way, might be enough."

Table of Contents

Levee 03

Brett Biebel

Brett Biebel teaches writing and literature at Augustana College in Rock Island, Illinois. His (mostly very) short fiction has appeared or is forthcoming in *Chautauqua, the minnesota review, Bridge Eight, Great River Review, The Masters Review,* and elsewhere. He is currently working on a collection of stories about football, masculinity, and the general state of the American Midwest. He can be reached at brettbiebel@augustana.edu.

Roadside America

Around about a year ago, I'm coming back from a job in Stapleton. Headed into town on 83, and this had to be November. Sometime between Cindy cutting bait and the rest of us getting Marietta to commit to *Heartland*. It's one of them nights you're surprised how dark it is at five o'clock. Windy too. Truck's veering a little toward the center line, and I'm trying not to overcorrect but I do and thank God for the rumble strip because there's a woman out there by herself on the shoulder with a camera hanging from her neck. And I mean a real camera. Got a flash bulb and everything. So I get safely by her, and I pull over. I'm thinking, what in the hell is she doing, the fucking nut? Could have been killed. Could get lost or snatched up by one of them long-hauls always coming through, and doesn't she watch the news? Maybe she's one of them artist types just don't know where she's at half the time, but Christ almighty, the sheer fucking ignorance. Somebody's got to enlighten her, and I take it upon myself. Start heading back to where she's standing, waving my arms a little so she knows I'm a man means no harm. "Ma'am," I say, but she just keeps on standing there, back to me, snapping away at some asphalt or gravel or prairie grass or what have you. But then I get a little closer, and I can see the side of her face, and this is important, alright? Is that she ain't pretty. Got short hair and one of them rat noses, and she ain't particularly ugly neither, but there's not much there for me if you understand so let's get that out of the way. But I see what she's taking pictures of, and it's a dead raccoon. Big fucker. Teeth hanging out, belly up. Must be pretty fresh because it ain't smell yet and I don't see no hawks circling. Little pools of blood barely dry too. I gotta be ten feet from her by now, and I don't want to scare the poor thing, so I stop.

"You alright there, miss?" I say, loud enough she has to hear, and she just puts her hand up. So I wait. She turns to face one of them gray sunsets and takes two more photos. Then, without even looking at me, she says, "Do you know how many animal carcasses there are on Nebraska highways at any given moment?"

Now, I don't have to tell you that I don't have the first, which is exactly what I tell her.

"Got to be hundreds," she says, "Maybe thousands."

"All in places no one should get stuck alone, I imagine," hoping she'll get the hint.

"What I want to do is photograph all of them. Every last one. Get as many as I can. Deer. Raccoons. Opossums. Squirrels, rabbits, skunks. Bears, if there's a car big enough. Or sandhill cranes or bobcats or coyotes or whatever else we got. Line them all up in this exact kind of light right here. Put them in nice even frames. Nice rows. Tic-tac-toe and death gets the square. I want to send the whole thing to *National Gerographic* and just call it 'America.' Just like that. I might even do one for each state, like with those quarters. People will want to collect the whole set."

The whole time she ain't looking at me. Just snapping away. Swear she was still going on about maybe buying out billboards or setting up a little roadside museum and so caught up she didn't even hear me going back to the truck. And as I drive away I'm looking at her in the rearview and watching her get smaller and knowing, Christ, the next time I run into something at 2 a.m. her face is gonna be the first thing on my mind and it couldn't have at least looked like Jolene from the Railway back when she was twenty-four? And it makes me an asshole, I know, but that's what I was thinking, and the shame of it is I ain't hit anything since and still can't stop thinking about her. Been driving around so much I got roadkill in my goddamn dreams. Just last week, you know Jimbo Larsen, lives out Homestead Road? He tells me he ran into a whitetail the night before on I-80, and what do I do but ask him where exactly and practically beg for the mile number so I can go out and have a look. I don't know if maybe I think she might be there or if it's some kind of same-place-different-time thrill I'm after, but I do. I go. Early morning, had to be 5, 6 a.m., and I find the spot alright, but the deer's gone. Don't know if the county came and got it or maybe some scavenger, but all I see is a few red stains. Big semis racing by and honking, and I'm on my knees feeling the pavement, and the whole thing must look ridiculous. It's cold, and I'm gulping coffee from a thermos too. Looking out, this field's got a layer of frost on it. A few trees in the distance. It's beautiful and brown and empty, and I must have hit the coffee too fast because I start to feel sick. My head is pounding, and I swear, I almost fucking hurled. But I didn't. I watched wind run across the prairie, and I somehow held it together. I somehow managed to keep it all in.

Megan Blankenship

Megan Blankenship is a sober hillbilly pianist, poet, and mystic from the Ozark Mountains. Last year, she spent six months alone in the wilds of Oregon as the 2018 Margery Davis Boyden Wilderness Writing Resident. Her poems have most recently appeared in *Poetry Northwest* and *Tar River Poetry*.

Another Bible Belt Origin Myth

Swallow the seeds,
a watermelon'll balloon
in your belly.
Our glutton mamas gobbled
too fast, failed
to spit them out.
Girl, beware: this
is what desire breeds.
Ask a class full of ten-
year-olds in Arkansas
to name the kinds of birds
they know, you'll run
out of room on the chalkboard.
One got so excited he threw in bees!
We were doing an exercise
on metaphor: my [emotion] is a [bird].
To tell you the truth,
I don't know when this fissure
cracked open inside me.

Robin Gow

Robin Gow is a poet, editor, and LGBTQ+ educator. He is the author of the chapbook *HONEYSUCKLE* by Finishing Line Press. His first full-length poetry collection is forthcoming with Tolsun Books, and his second is forthcoming with Weasel Press. They have facilitated LGBTQ+ inclusivity trainings for universities and healthcare networks across the country. He is a graduate student and professor at Adelphi University.

Séance

We come with shovels—
          jabbing them into the dining room table.

What is left to talk about if I don't talk about
          the body?   If there is no body
                    to discuss.

There is soil in every object just
beneath the moist surface.

          Fingernails on my throat—
I spit my dirt into the cosmos

          a dropped pot of skeletons.

We have a fire escape we could
cover with herbs.   A rose bush

          sprouting from the only way out.

Shovels and spades and rakes.

Kissing a mirror not out of vanity
but to tell the creatures in there
          to come out.

Is this the first time you've tried
to talk to the dead?

I set leeks out on the kitchen table.
Before my grandmother was dead
I pretended she was because
that was easier.

What must that be like—to be
the grandmother of a black hole—

What does she know
about me that I could never
see for myself.

Coming to terms with being
the only creature
            still pouring with thought

I plea with ghosts
to tell me a story—to throw glasses
            down on the floor.

I want a poltergeist—
I want a possession.

Here there are my limbs what
will you make of them.

        So so much dirt.

Cannibalism of a memory
you play back to yourself
            on video tape.

Hold hands with ghosts—fingers
       cold and nervous

a link—a soft chain.

Ghosts asking ghosts
asking ghosts—
        how far down does this go?

A List of Tattoos I Want to Get

Worms on my ankles.

A fly behind my ear.

An acorn on my tongue.

Yes, they do tattoos there.

Portrait of myself as a baby on my stomach. Black/white. Eyes slightly askew. Mouth
    a warble.

        They can never quite replicate a photograph.

        It's also as if skin rejects carrying

        the likeness of another body.

Roller skate. Just one. On my throat.

Wine bottle on my throat.

Bendy straw also on my throat.

        There's a lot more room than it seems

when you really think about it.

Gumballs on the thighs.

        Spilling.

Leviticus 20:13 circling my anus.

Teddy bear on my forearm.

Goggle eyes under my real eyes.

A quote from a favorite book in cursive across my back.

        Give me a quote you like—

        make it a good one.

DO NOT RESUSITATE around my hips.

        Synonym for let me die right now if you find me.

        A good joke when someone tries to go down on me

        and finds nothing down there but reeking fears.

Thunder on my eyelids.

Rotting cucumbers on my collarbone. Two of them.

Match sticks on each of my fingers besides my thumbs.

Tulip bulbs on my thumbs.

A scream on my lips and around my eyes.

The sound of the train calling for a dead friend on the tops of my feet.

A portrait of myself three genders thinner on my ribs.

      I'll make her dance.

Buttons all over so that a lover might count them in bed, saying softly *one, two,*

    three—another!

Crying on my calves.

Sobbing on my thighs.

      There's so much room.

The Moon Tarot Card on my thigh too.

Someone else's thumb print over my own.

Someone else's name on the roof of my mouth so I say it instead of my own.

The same thumb tulip, dead now, on my forehead.

      Why would you put something right there forever?
         Because that's how it ends.

Keith Edward Vaughn

Keith Edward Vaughn was born in Chattanooga, Tennessee. He holds an MFA in Painting from the Cranbrook Academy of Art. He has published art criticism in *Carla* and fiction in the *Angel City Review*. His writing is also featured in Faith Wilding's *Fearful Symmetries* from Intellect Books, Ltd. He lives and works in Alameda, California.

The Wet Season

My feet are propped on the penthouse balcony railing of Star Fish Plaza, a Brutalist condominium tower ringed by palm trees that pin down a flap of Guam's western coast. "Private Eyes" by Hall and Oates is on, again, the extreme volume muffled by sliding glass doors. The album is such an anomaly in my biological father's collection of big band and original cast recordings, I assume it was lent or left behind by a visitor—maybe his last. I open a can of Budweiser, my first of the day, and read what little I wrote yesterday—two-and-a-half scribbled pages of aimless dialogue between the man with two heads and the lady from the Institute.

> *Are you sure this is a good idea?*
> *Man, I ain't sure of nothin'.*
> *It doesn't have to be a good idea. It's good optics for the Institute—and that means funding.*

I don't know where to go from there. As convenient as it would be to blame my hangover and the oppressive humidity, I know it's because I don't know what my story is about. That it doesn't matter makes me feel better and worse at the same time.

Just like the last three days, I woke up jetlagged, hungover, and disoriented in my father's California King to a new round of text messages, DMs, and Instagram posts from Rob. Yesterday there were dispatches from his and "his" son's excursions to the Santa Monica Pier and The Getty. The day before that, it was Universal Studios. Today, it was Rob and Augustus at the La Brea Tar Pits. The kid had chocolate ice cream—I hope that's what it was—all over his face, making it hard to tell if any resemblance is developing…

> *Gusty asked if the dinosaurs are real! I explained that they are sculptures and 'real' insofar as they exist—*

Gusty? I deleted everything without reply.

I thumb sweat off my upper lip, toss the legal pad aside, flip a bug off my bare chest, drain the Budweiser, and stand, woozy. Over the balcony, I see Young, the groundskeeper, carrying his five-gallon bucket across the patchy lawn, looking over both shoulders like a cartoon crook making off with the loot. He sneaks down the steps to the beach.

Sliding open the glass doors, Hall and Oates and glacial air conditioning wash over me. Until four days ago, no one had been inside my father's condo since he left it thirty-five years hence, expecting to return in eleven—eight with good behavior. The sports and porn magazines on the coffee table date to August 1982. There are bottles of sour wine and spoiled Scotch behind the padded bar. On top is a brown glass ashtray from the Tumon Bay Racquet Club with two Winston butts in it, one of them tipped with hot pink lipstick. The rosewood-paneled walls are clustered with pictures of my father and the various semi-pro tennis players he coached before he did his little trick.

We bear a slight resemblance.

An open shelving unit divides the living and dining areas. The only things on it are hardback copies of *The Ultimate Tennis Book*, *The Joy of Sex*, and *The Year Book of World Tennis* for the year 1972—the year I was born—and paperbacks of *Carrie*, *Jaws*, *The Exorcist*, *Lucifer's Hammer*, and *Helter Skelter*, all of them dog-eared, none past page 122.

Haggar suits and Fila sportswear hang in the closets. Mirrored bases make the bed and nightstands look like they're floating above the burgundy shag carpeting that runs throughout the condo, including the bathrooms where vinyl wallpaper printed with gilt bamboo branches peels back from black tile. The toilets and sinks are also black. The toiletries in the medicine cabinet—Right Guard, Skin Bracer, Listerine—have crazily low Kmart price tags.

The Betamax porn tapes in the credenza are another matter. Some of those have eighty- and ninety-dollar price tags. And for only *two hours* of content. The twenty-four-inch RCA television and the Toshiba ViewStar Betamax player still work. My second night in the penthouse I watched as much as I could stand of *Bra-Busting Abductions*. One of the girls had tits like Karen's and once the novelty of seeing them bound in duct tape cooled, I pressed Stop, more bummed out than turned on. I tried the July '82 *Hustler* but ended up falling asleep reading a profile of Merle Haggard called "From Convict to Country King."

#

I've only known about the condo since last year when my mother called to tell me the bad news about Chuck, my first and favorite stepdad.

"They scattered his ashes at El Segundo Beach," she had said. "God only knows why. I can think of nicer beaches."

"I can't believe you didn't tell me sooner," I said. "I would have gone to the service. There are nicer beaches, sure, but he was from El Segundo."

"Oh please. Did he tell you that? Chuck was from Hawthorne, just like Caroline. You know, I just found out she dated your father—your biological father—right before he did his little trick."

That's how my mother refers to my biological father's disappearance to Guam in the late summer of 1977. We had no idea where he was until he died of a heart attack eight years later in Hagåtña Detention Facility.

At the end of a rant I hadn't paid any attention to, my mother mentioned Star Fish Plaza as if I'd heard of it. I pretended I had.

"I would advise you to sell it," she said, "except it's probably not worth anything. Not in US dollars anyway."

"I'm pretty sure Guam is on the dollar," I said.

"The whole place is overrun with snakes. I guess that's why your father liked it."

Ten months after that conversation, Rob called. I let it go to voicemail.

Hey, man. Hope you're well. Augustus and I are coming to LA in September to celebrate his fifth birthday with his grandparents... with uh, Karen's mom and dad. They've been really great through everything. Really supportive... Anyway, uh... I'd love to see you and—

I pressed Delete and called a real estate lawyer.

#

When the elevator doors shudder open on the ground floor, a sickly floral perfume pinches my nose. The building manager, Felicia, is standing in her usual spot beside the bust of Venus in the lobby, staring through the glass doors that open onto the courtyard.

"*Hafa adai*," she says when she catches me in her periphery.

"Hi." I refuse to attempt the customary Chamorro greeting.

Felicia is wearing a sleeveless floral print dress. Her pedicured feet are squeezed into puce zories—flip-flops in the rest of the world—that match her lipstick and eye shadow.

"You're up early today," she says. It's 2:30 p.m. "You're getting used to Guam time."

"Heaven help me." Under my arm I have the legal pad and four cans of Budweiser wrapped in one of my father's Ocean Pacific beach towels. I'm wearing a pair of his trunks and his Foster Grant sunglasses.

"How is the man with two heads doing?" Felicia asks.

"Uh, just great."

On my arrival at Star Fish Plaza, I told Felicia I have a development deal with Netflix for a series about a man with two heads—one black and one white—and that I had come here to write, free from distraction. She had grabbed my arm and squealed and told me how much she loved *Stranger Things*, but that she had never heard of *Sunset Strippers*—my last job, a reality show about Hollywood pole dancers. I don't hold it against her. It only aired seven episodes.

"When *Stranger Things* is on, that's the only time my husband and kids can tolerate being in the same room together," she had said, her eyes twinkling with the crucifix at her fleshy throat, "not like when they were young. Mary Katherine just turned thirteen and Peter is—"

"Awesome," I said. "My show is like *Stranger Things* meets *The Thing with Two Heads*. Ever see that? 1972, with Ray Milland and Rosie Greer?" Of course she hadn't. "Anyway, a white guy's head gets grafted onto a black guy's body, and a lady from the institute that performed the operation takes them around to speaking engagements and tries to keep them from bickering. It's all about race and diversity and whatever."

Now, as I'm trying to get past her to the pool, she says, "I can just see you out on the balcony, writing and living that oceanfront lifestyle."

"Uh-huh. I was doing that very thing earlier." I angle my body toward the doors.

"Going to the pool?" asks Felicia, eyeing the bundle under my arm.

"Trying to," I say, taking another sidestep.

"Star Fish Plaza was built in 1975." She sweeps her arm in a rainbow arc, deodorant caked in her stubbly armpit. "All the fixtures that you see are original."

"No kidding." I give an obliging look around at the split plaster, loose switch plates, mailbox doors that don't latch, chipped tile, and sticky elevator doors. All of the dome-shaped skylights are cracked. I reach around Felicia for a tarnished door handle.

"The architect was a genius," she says, blocking my way. "Building materials were chosen for their harmonious relationship to the environment."

"You can't go wrong with stucco and glass," I say.

"Just steps to the beach, Star Fish Plaza gives you that coastal living experience you've always dreamed of, with ocean views and plenty of stucco and glass—"

I push past her and out into the wet wool climate.

#

Yesterday, just so Felicia would shut up, I braved the rotting planks that lead to the beach. Picking my way across the narrow strip of rocks and mud, I stepped on the writhing tail of a reddish-brown snake that had been neatly cut in two. The head was hanging over a rock a few feet away, nodding in the low tide, eyes rolled back and jaws still biting. I wanted to crush it to make them stop, but I was barefoot. Hardly the coastal living experience Felicia, for some reason, thinks I've been dreaming of.

#

Poolside, the beers and I are sweating. I peel off my shirt and open a can. Two of the ten Pool Rules posted on the gate are that alcohol and people under its influence are prohibited. But, as with the volume of the stereo in the penthouse, there's never anyone around to object. In four days, I haven't seen anyone in the pool, either jacuzzi, or the weight room. No one ever plays on any of the four tennis courts, or putts on the synthetic greens. Even the placid bay and the sandy beaches spread at the feet of the resorts to the tonier north are deserted.

The pool is so warm there is no shock when I dive in. After a few laps, I get out, blot my face dry, and flip open the legal pad. The lady from the Institute is trying to keep the peace between the two heads.

Why can't we wear some of my clothes for a change? asks the white head. I'm imaging a Steve Carell type.

Because they're out of style and they won't fit me, says the black one—

somebody big, like Ving Rhames, but younger and more handsome. *Don't forget, you're the guest here.*

Hurry up and find a compromise, says the lady. *We're running late.* I picture a hapless but sexy Alison Brie type with bigger tits. Karen would have been perfect...

With absolutely no idea where to go, I open another beer and stare at the glaring yellow page. "I Can't Go for That (No Can Do)" keeps running through my head. It's maddening. Since I got here, despite—or maybe because of—the solitude and the drinking, it's been a struggle to focus. Sparing me the bother, a mechanical snarl rips the tropical quietude.

I bolt upright as Young comes around the corner of the building in a face mask and goggles. He's swinging a gas-powered leaf blower over the unhealthy, but completely leaf-free, lawn. I pound the rest of my beer and open another, drinking half of it in an angry gulp.

For what has to be ten minutes I watch this idiot wave the roaring leaf blower, aiming at nothing, loping in circles like a junkie. For some reason, I think of Rob and Karen, the way they looked when I saw each of them last, in tears.

This... you... it was all a mistake, and I hate myself for what I've done to him, she had said. *Please, don't ever—*

The leaf blower screams, takes a breath, and screams again higher, louder.

My hammering pulse makes my hands shake. I pound the last beer and kick the empty cans into the pool. Dizzy, I gather my shirt, towel and legal pad, and let the gate slam behind me, in violation of the final Pool Rule.

"*Hafa adai!*" says Felicia, standing beside Venus.

"What's with the leaf blower?" I ask, practically yelling.

"Ah. His name is Young. He does a great job of keeping Star Fish Plaza clean and well-main—"

"He showed up with the leaf blower as soon as I—"

"Yes," says Felicia. "I hear it."

"I hope you do. It's really loud, besides being totally pointless. There are no leaves out there."

"I know." Felicia preens. "Young does a great job of keeping Star Fish Plaza clean and—"

"There are *no leaves to begin with.*"

Felicia's grin wavers. "The property is very clean and well-maintained. You um, get that resort-style living experience with all the amenities on your list of must-haves, including kidney-shaped swimming pool the kids will love, two jacuzzis, synthetic putting greens, and four tennis courts."

"My *list*? What do you mean? I don't have any kids." My head buzzes, picturing Augustus, his face obscured by filth. "And I know all about the amenities," I look down at my father's dripping trunks and back at Felicia, "obviously. Look, just tell what's-his-face to hold the leaf blowing if he sees me out there." I hold up the damp legal pad. "I was right in the middle of a very emotional scene—the emotional core of the whole story. I came here to work, you know, free from distraction."

"He has to do it during the day," Felicia says.

"But he's not *doing anything* except making noise."

"Later, there are snakes everywhere."

After a beat, less strident, I say, "Yeah, I've heard that about this place."

#

Later, when I wake up, it could be dawn or dusk. The light under the drapes is blue. My temples throb. It hurts to swallow. I reach for my phone. 1 p.m. Six new texts from Rob. The first one includes a picture of the bastard kid, his face gory with pizza sauce, standing between a six-foot Elmo and a paunchy Spider-Man in front of Grauman's Chinese Theatre.

Gusty says Elmo smells like—

I can guess. I delete all the messages without reading further.

Karen was always suggestible but how in the world could she have agreed to the name Augustus?

Heavy clouds had settled over the island in the night, and it's slightly cooler than usual on the balcony. Slightly. I open a beer, yesterday's take-out, and the legal pad. I don't remember writing the last couple of pages. It looks like I named the characters. Cool.

Don't nobody got time for that, says Bob, on the phone with Carol, in crude imitation of Cordarius.

Man, is that s'posed to be me? Cordarius asks. *I don't sound like that.*

19

Listen, whoever-this-is, says Carol, *you're due at the elementary school at one o'clock. So be dressed and ready to go when I get there.*

A sharp gust of wind blows the beer can and take-out container off the table. Suds, chicken bones, and pickled mango fly all over me and the legal pad. I curse and jump to my feet. Below, I see Young skulking across the dim grass, carrying a shovel in both hands like a rifle. Rain is spitting fat drops on my bare, curling toes. Young stops, and raises the shovel over his head. The wind rushes. He drives the blade into the ground. Again. And once again.

He picks up one twisting half of an orange snake, maybe two feet long, and throws it over the edge of the land, into the thundering surf. He does the same with the head connected to another lashing foot-and-a-half, holding it in such a way that he isn't bitten, like he's done it before. Rain surges. He sprints for the tower.

My face is wet.

Back inside the arctic time capsule, wondering what to do with myself other than get drunk listening to "Private Eyes", I consider giving *Bra-Busting Abductions* another try because no writing is getting done today. I can already tell.

The elevator stops on the penthouse floor—the only time in five days it has. I hear the doors rattle open. A slapping sound approaches my door. Zories. Felicia. I muffle the opening crack of a beer can with an orange velvet throw pillow, waiting for her knock so I can ignore it. She slap-slap-slaps past the door, leaving the sounds of wind and rain.

I ease the door open and Felicia's cloying perfume grabs my face. At the end of the hall, the door to the other penthouse is standing open. I creep toward the darkness inside.

Though the condo is empty, I can see it is only half as dated as my father's. The stainless sink, black kitchen appliances, and granite countertops are the only hints as to how the yawning, gray-tiled space was once divided.

Felicia stands at the far wall, smoking and staring out the sliding glass doors. She jumps and drops her cigarette when she notices me and does a little cha-cha when it falls on her toes. She stomps on the butt like it was bug and smiles, embarrassment coloring her cheeks above the heavy rouge and under the running mascara.

"*Hafa adai.*"

"I'm sorry I startled you," I say, tasting a fog of smoke and perfume. "I hate to be startled. I should have knocked." All true. "I uh, noticed the door was open, and I remembered how you said this unit was unoccupied, so I just… well, anyway, I'll let you get back to… whatever." I turn to go. She stops me.

"This unit has three bedrooms, two baths, and great ocean views," she faces the deluge, "ordinarily. It offers that open-concept living experience at a price-point that's within your budget."

"Huh? I don't get it," I say. "I'm not buying a condo. I have one. You know that."

"Oh, I know." She sighs and her voice is weaker on the other side of it. "I just love this property. I love being here and talking about it. It makes me feel like I'm… somewhere else, somewhere… not real, like I'm on HGTV, on a show like *Island Hunters* or *Beachfront Bargain Hunt*…. Until you moved in, nobody had been on this floor in fifteen years. That's why I come here to smoke. So I don't bother anybody. Today, I'm not so lucky."

"It's okay," I say, looking at the mashed cigarette. "I hope that wasn't your last one."

She shakes her head.

"And I didn't really move in," I say. "I'm going back to LA as soon as I finish the script." This is untrue. I'm leaving as soon as I can.

Felicia's tattooed eyebrows jump. She clutches my arm in her clammy hands, digging in her nails, which are painted with tropical sunsets complete with silhouetted palm trees and Golden Arches-shaped seagulls.

"What happens to the two-headed man?" she asks. "I promise not to tell anyone—not even my family. We never talk to each other anymore… please."

"He, uh… well, he…" I shake my head. "Nothing happens to him. I don't have a deal with Netflix or anybody else. I came all the way here to avoid seeing this guy—an old friend, actually. I slept with his dead wife. I mean, she was alive when I slept with her. Obviously. Anyway, she's dead now, and there's a kid, and I've done the math and… well, you get it."

Felicia releases my arm. Her face and shoulders fall. A buffet of rain pelts the glass doors like gravel flung by the wheels of a getaway car.

"Yes, I get it." Her false eyelashes twitch like the legs of dying spiders. "This is the wet season. The only people here now have to be."

The next day, I wake before noon with an instant grasp of my surroundings and without a hangover. The light under the drapes is yellow. I throw them open. Last night's storm has already turned to shimmering steam. I pick up my phone and scroll past a stream of Rob's Instagram posts: the kid with mustard on his face at Dodger's Stadium, grimacing and picking the seat of his pants at the Griffith Observatory, in Karen's parents' backyard in the Valley, eyes shut tight, mouth and nostrils impacted with blue icing. It's impossible to tell who he looks like.

#birthdayboy #nofilter

As usual, there are also texts and DMs from Rob.

Gusty said the colors of the sunset remind him of his mom. I told him how much she loved him and—

Delete.

There is also a new voicemail. My heart beats faster and my thumb trembles over the red Delete button. For some reason, I relent and listen.

Hey, man. It's Rob. I don't know whether or not you've been getting my messages, but Gusty and I have been having a great time. I'm just sorry we didn't get to see you. We're headed back to Denver tomorrow morning... so, next time, hopefully... I, uh... I hope you haven't been avoiding me because of what happened between you and Karen. She told me all about it when she was in the hospital, and it's—I'm not mad... maybe I should be, but... I just don't want to lose both of you, you know? My world is getting so small... you loved her too. You know how beautiful she was and how much she—

But I hadn't loved her. I hit Delete and call the airport. "Private Eyes" blares as I pack.

Josh Bettinger

Josh Bettinger is a poet and editor. He is the author of the chapbook *A Dynamic Range Of Various Designs For Quiet*, from *GASHER*. Recent publications include *Salt Hill Journal*, *Western Humanities Review*, *Handsome Poetry*, *SLICE*, *flock*, *Columbia Journal*, *Atlas Review*, *Crazyhorse*, and *Boston Review*, among others. He lives in Northern California with his wife and kids.

Some Land, Some Place, America 2019

The ants came up
through wet floorboards like a drunken
Holofernes, but

this is not a metaphor: my house
is drifting into a bog of the humors.

I thought we might inch away
in a dinghy
of rainwater and squirrels, yet

the hours tacked at us—
all the elements
of a good story put to bed with a newly installed
thermostat. I loved

the sharp teeth
you'd shown
and I love the sharp heart
you wield, in a home that shuffles along fault
lines and reeks

of some otherness purchase:
what begins always beginning, what stays
always staying, what loves
always loving: something that

can actually sleep
at night, blessing the wisteria

we've unearthed. See—it's not all
bad: the neighbors
rising up in their tonics alight

burning fragrant
to meet us like old dogs in the street
as if they know we're not here to hurt them.

Jar Full Of Moon On A Highway In The Sun

A peach striation on the blue wall means
that just beyond the crack of the door
there is something different. Perhaps

a repetition of skins, maybe a meaningless disaster,
potentially the rictus of Death waiting

to swallow us whole—a fiction of hearts to drown.

Whatever it is it coats me like sweat. Whatever
it isn't is debatable like the retreat of trees

in the mirror when we stand silently at it.
Stop pretending that what we're owed isn't everything.

Mark Robinson

Mark Robinson earned his BA in English Literature from the University of Iowa and is an MFA candidate at Lindenwood University. His poems have appeared in *The Red Flag Poetry Postcard Series*, *Naugatuck River Review*, and *Bending Genres*. His chapbook *Just Last Days* will appear in Summer 2020. Mark currently lives in West Des Moines, Iowa with his wife Jen and their children Lyla, Aya, Liam, Cora, and Minni.

Mountainside in September

Up here you can catch
at just that delicate moment
the perfect brilliance of bright yellow Aspen leaves
dotting the deep evergreen mountainside.

In a long white coat, a faceless surgeon
explains the fiery spotting on a scan of my lungs
and a plan for numbing my body
enough to cut into the healthy flesh
to remove the ravishing pits.

My chest glowing coals, I celebrate those colors
that overtake summer's shiny green leaves:
the yellows, the oranges,
and the reds that must drop soon
lest their fluid freeze
damaging them beyond use.

Jakob Bailey

Jakob Bailey is a fiction writer from Nashville, Tennessee. While home, he spends time working in multiple writing groups, reading for *CRAFT Magazine*, and hosting large dinner parties. In the morning, with coffee, Jakob reads the classics and unpublished work.

In A Wall

I was sitting at a bar in Boston, slowly working my way through a watered-down Negroni, when I first heard about the Wall-People. The atmosphere was quiet. Only background music played. I was still dressed for work but my tie was loose and the top button on my shirt was undone. A tall woman sat at a table behind me, a whispering man sat beside her. Across the bar a lonely-looking bartender with a long face wiped glasses. The whole place felt distant. Like a spot reserved for the elite and couples with lusty affairs.

Inside my head, I played around with the phrase Wall-Person, mining rocks in search of some diamond—some insight—but nothing came.

"Wall-Person?" I said.

"You've never seen one?" my friend asked. Her name was Liz and she was a friend of my ex. Anytime she passed through Boston we'd normally get together. We had a totally platonic relationship, and over the course of the few years we've known each other neither of us had done anything to change that.

I twisted the straw in my drink and stabbed at my ice a couple times. "Never even heard of them."

She stared at me like I was trying to trick her into admitting something she kept carefully guarded. She wore a long black dress better suited for a funeral than a bar. I waited for her to continue and realized the Negroni was making its way into my head. The light behind the bar started to twinkle with the bliss of pre-intoxication.

Liz leaned back in her seat. "I've only seen them twice," she said. "The first time was in high school. It was after a school basketball game, and I was tossing clothes from my locker into my gym bag. I'd made a few bad calls during the game and I was reflecting on that, I wasn't really paying attention to anything, just thinking. But then I heard someone breathing, and on the wall by the water fountain I saw a Wall-Person. He wasn't looking at me, in fact it seemed like he didn't know I was there at all. Seeing him made my spine to shiver. Right here," she said, pointing at her lower spine. "I quickly grabbed my bag and ran off."

I took a sip of my Negroni while I thought. "What does a Wall-Person look like?" I asked, unsure what to make of her story.

She swished her glass around. "I don't know how to describe them," she said. "Picture someone half stuck in a wall and half not, like they're trapped or melting. The one I saw at my high school was standing in profile, like that famous silhouette of Alfred Hitchcock, you know the one I'm talking about?"

I nodded.

"Like that," she said. "He was split right down the middle. I couldn't get a good view of his face because of it. He didn't look sad or anything, he just kept looking. His eyes danced all over the place. It was really freaky."

"Sounds freaky," I said.

"It wasn't until last week that I saw another one." She looked away from me, then back down to her Old Fashioned, which she oscillated before finishing. "I was leaving a grocery store and I'd parked close to the entrance. I tossed my groceries into the passenger seat and started my car, and when I clicked on the headlights I could see one on the side of the grocery store. It was like before, half of him was in the wall and the other half wasn't, but this time he was looking straight ahead. I could see him perfectly. And maybe it was because I was in a car and that gave me a sense of comfort, but I didn't feel the urge to run away. Don't get me wrong, I was scared. But I wanted to really see what I was seeing, you know?"

I nodded, "Sure," I said.

"But after staring at him for a while I realized he couldn't see me. I could look at him, but his eyes never looked at me. He looked past me, all around me. He stared at my car, the cars next to me, he studied everything—but he never looked at me. Strange, right?"

I shrugged, "It all sounds strange to me."

"Yeah, I guess so," she said. "But the strangest thing was that, as I stared at the Wall-Person, I realized another thing. I knew him. It took a long time before the memory came back to me, but once it clicked into place I was certain of it. He was my next-door neighbor when I was a kid. I'd totally forgotten about him, and once he moved away I never saw him again. Which isn't particularly weird, we weren't close, just two people that lived next to each other—and to be honest I can't even remember his name, but there he was. Half stuck in a wall on the side of a grocery store."

Liz tapped her glass on the bar top once to shake her ice loose, then took a piece and placed it in her mouth. I thought about her story. In my experience, Liz wasn't the type to make things up. She was normally very dry and factual. That's part of why I enjoyed her company. She was always to the point, as far back as I knew her. My ex,

Anna, and her were roommates in college. Liz watched our relationship come and go, and Anna eventually moved out west. We dated on and off for two years, but decided to call it quits. It was weird that neither Liz nor I spoke to her anymore, but here Liz and I were, connected through her and talking years afterward. It's hard to tell who'll stick in your life. Like throwing random knives in the dark and hoping that one will hit something.

Eventually I asked, "Do you think he was an illusion of some type?" Not fully sure where to go from there.

"No," she answered quickly. "I don't know how I know that, but I do. He wasn't an illusion, or a spirit. He was a Wall-Person, through and through."

"Then what do you think they are?" I asked.

She sighed. "I'm not really sure, but I've been thinking about it. What if they're people that have disappeared from our lives, the ones that we'll never see again—bank tellers, friends from kindergarten, everyone's lives are filled with people that they'll likely never see again, and they have to go somewhere, right?"

"Mhmm," I said, amazed at how similar our minds were.

"Well, what if they become Wall-People? They melt into the wall and disappear from our thoughts and lives. You can't even remember them until they appear again, somewhere in the physical world and stuck in a wall."

"Makes you wonder," I said, and finished the last of my Negroni.

It was two in the morning before we left the bar. The moon was hidden behind long dark clouds. Outside we hugged and Liz called for a ride. My head was fuzzy and I decided to walk home; I didn't live far and I could collect my car in the morning. Along the way I thought about what Liz had told me. I tried my best to picture everyone I'd ever come across, but of course it was pointless. Too many people come and go, pass us on the street, quit jobs, have kids. Life moves fast even when we're not paying attention.

A few cars passed me while I walked, and each one sounded like a vacuum losing power as it sped by. A dog that I couldn't see barked for what felt like a lifetime. The night air cleared my head and the high I'd been riding from the alcohol was slipping away. It was chilly and bound to rain. I picked up my pace and was home in a short amount of time.

Once inside I collapsed on my couch and clicked on the TV. A news story began about a man who quit his job and started an oyster farm. The man on the TV was middle-aged and his skin had a leathery look to it. As if he was only borrowing it for the time being. His eyes were blue and he talked at length about his oysters, and the challenges they possessed. "You have to keep an eye on your oysters. If you let your guard down even for a second they'll overtake you," he said. Unintentionally, I pictured all the terrible things oysters could do in the shadows, unwatched and free.

The news report reminded me of a girl I dated who loved oysters. She told me she could eat oysters everyday. For breakfast, lunch, and dinner. I hated them. The texture was too much, that slimy brine. She'd slurp them down, one after the other, like the world might run out at any second. Her breath smelled terrible afterward. Her oyster consumption played a part in our separation. A weird thing to take into account, but we can't choose what bothers us. Maybe that's what the man on the TV meant about letting your guard down around oysters: they'll ruin love.

That night I saw a Wall-Person. I don't know what caused it, or why now, so soon after Liz told me about them. Maybe I needed to hear their name first? Or maybe it was like hearing a new word, and then all of a sudden hearing that word everywhere. Regardless, when I awoke later that night the cloudy sky had transformed into an inky blackness and raindrops lightly dotted my window. I sat up and rubbed my eyes. The TV was still playing, and on the screen a woman wearing a purple dress pointed at a small car. Stumbling in the light of the TV, I made my way to the bathroom to go pee. When I was finishing up, something popped right at eye-level like the flash of a silver coin at the bottom of a long dark well, and coming out of the wall above my toilet was a Wall-Person.

I couldn't see the Wall-Person clearly, but I could tell it was a woman. The wall started right at the bottom of her ribcage and her body seemed to be leaning forward out of the wall. Her right shoulder was exposed, along with her right arm; her left was still submerged in the plaster. Long brown hair was carefully pulled to the back of her head. She looked to be in her late thirties or early forties. Her eyes moved all around but nothing else, like she was frozen, held in place by the wall. At first I couldn't move either, both of us frozen in place; then, regaining myself, I clicked on the light.

She didn't look to be upset that she was trapped in the wall, almost like someone who was in the middle of a step forward when a wall solidified around them and they've yet to take notice. Her eyes darted around, but she never looked toward me. Watching her, I took notice that she was quite pretty and well-dressed. Like a business woman on her way home from the office. My heart kept beating, but the longer I stared at the Wall-Person, the calmer I became.

After a few deep breaths I said, "Hello?" almost to myself.

"Hello?" the Wall-Person said back, her voice like a soft whisper. Her mouth only opened slightly to make a sound.

Hearing her speak caused me to lose my nerve again, and I was quiet, unable to say anything.

The Wall-Person's eyes moved all over the bathroom, refusing to stay still. "Can you hear me?" the Wall-Person asked, and I felt a kick in my stomach.

"Yes," I said.

"Where am I?"

"You're in my bathroom," I said.

"Pardon?" she said.

"I said 'You're in my bathroom.'"

"I don't think that's true," the Wall-Person said.

I waved my hand in front of her face. "Can you see anything?" I asked.

Her eyes rolled. "Of course," she said back.

"Can you see me?"

"Only barely," she said. "But you're getting clearer."

I wasn't sure what that meant. My legs went numb and my head was spinning. I slowly sank down to the ground, propping my back against the sink on the opposite side of the bathroom.

"Are you still there?" the Wall-Person asked.

"Yes," I said. "I'm sitting down now, my knees felt weak."

"Oh," she said in that soft voice.

I pulled my knees up to my chest and rested my head on them, staring up at the Wall-Person. Was it normal for Wall-People to talk? My knowledge on the subject was far from the best. Looking back, I should've asked Liz more questions. I studied the woman's face. She seemed like a perfectly normal person, other than a wall running through her. She had a sharp jawline and her mouth formed a thin straight line. I could only see one of her ears (the other was stuck in the wall) and it was pale, like a newborn baby, and a small dot stood out on her earlobe where an earring would normally hang.

"My friend told me about you," I said. "Earlier tonight."

"About me?"

"About Wall-People," I corrected.

Staying perfectly still, the Wall-Person asked, "What did she tell you?"

"That you're not spirits, or illusions," I said.

"What do you think?"

"I don't know yet."

The Wall-Person was silent.

"Where did you come from?"

She sighed. "Same place as everyone, I guess." Her voice took on a sour tone like I was wasting her time.

"How did you end up in my wall?" I asked.

"From my perspective I'm not in any wall."

I thought about this for a second. "Can you describe what you see?"

"It's like looking through water, or floating in space," she said. "Nothing around me looks real."

I tapped my toes on the ground. The cold bathroom floor helped ground me to reality. "Do you have a family?" I asked.

"I have a husband," the Wall-Person said.

I tried to picture her with a husband, two Wall-People trapped together, but my head started to hurt. "What does your husband do?" I asked, fumbling for questions.

"Nothing, he stays at home. I'm the one who works," the Wall-Person said.

"What do you do?" I asked.

"I buy and sell used cars."

"Hmmm."

"What about you?" the Wall-Person asked.

"I'm a copywriter," I said. "I work for a pasta company."

The Wall-Person smiled for the first time. It appeared strange to see someone smile while stuck in a wall. Like they thought of a joke and refused to share it.

"What's something you wrote about pasta?"

I had to think, then said, "'Try our new linguine, delicious golden brown noodles made only with the finest ingredients. Pan served, boiled, or baked, our linguine will have your family begging for more.'"

The Wall-Person said nothing.

"Or something to that effect," I added.

"And that sells pasta?" the Wall-Person asked.

"Normally, but everyone's a critic."

We sat in silence. I tapped my toes on the ground. The Wall-Person's eyes kept looking all around. I grew thirsty and asked if she'd like anything to drink. She said no, so I ran to the kitchen and poured myself a glass of water before returning to the bathroom. I sat back down against the sink and watched the Wall-Person for some time. Everything in my bathroom was normal—the shower, the toilet, towels hanging on hooks, nothing out of place—except for a person wedged in my wall.

"My friend thinks that you might be someone I've met at one point in my life and have forgotten about," I said suddenly.

The Wall-Person sighed. "Your friend sounds like quite the expert."

I took a long sip of water. "She knows more than I do," I said, setting my glass down. "Is it painful?"

"What?"

"Being in a wall."

"I just feel numb. And sleepy."

"You can go if you'd like," I said.

She smiled. "I don't think that's how it works."

"We just have to wait it out, you mean?"

"Yes. We just have to wait."

I took in every detail of the Wall-Person, trying to piece together if I'd seen her before, but nothing came to mind. To me she was just another random individual. Someone that could have easily been at home right now, lying in her own bed dreaming of selling cars next to her sleeping husband. How was it that she came to be in my wall? All of a sudden it seemed cruel. Like a bad prank.

"Where were you before you came here?" I asked.

"I was on my way home from the supermarket. I was going to make spaghetti tonight."

I took another sip of water to clear my throat. "What's the last thing you remember?" I asked.

"Hmm," she seemed to think. "Getting on the subway. I remember because a man gave up his seat to let me sit down."

"And they say chivalry is dead," I said. The Wall-Person smiled. "Anything else?"

"Let me think. We arrived at my stop and I got off the subway. The next thing I remember is boiling water for the spaghetti. I was watching small bubbles form on the bottom of the pot, each one growing until it shot upward and exploded on the surface. I remember thinking about how much pasta I should make for just me and my husband, and as the water started to turn to a rolling boil I looked back into the pot and that's when I saw you. And now here we are," the Wall-Person said.

"Just like that?"

"Just like that."

I ran through a quick mental checklist of what the Wall-Person told me. "Any idea of what pasta you used?"

"No. Why?"

"I'm just grasping at straws. Making mountains out of molehills." I rose to my feet. "I'm going to get you out of that wall," I said suddenly.

The Wall-Person coughed. "How?"

"I'll pull you out. Can you grab my arm?"

"I can't move at all."

I walked close to the Wall-Person and really looked at her. She seemed totally normal, her skin reflected the light slightly. The wall appeared like it was built around her. Or she was built in the wall. The two were inseparable now, as if they belonged together and without her there the whole building would come tumbling down. I reached out and took her hand. Her body felt warm and soft. She breathed in when our skin touched, and her eyes locked onto mine for the first time.

"I can see you clearly now," she said. "I can see everything."

"I'm going to try pulling you out of the wall," I said.

A thin layer of water formed at the bottom of her eyes. "Please don't," she said. "I want to go home now. Just leave me be, it'll all be over in the morning."

I let go of her hand and it dropped toward the ground like gravity had a vendetta against it. "Are you sure?" I asked.

"Yes," she said. "Get some sleep."

I turned to go but she called me back, "Can you please turn the light off?" she asked.

"Sure," I said, and clicked it off. The bathroom was left in darkness, and the only way I knew she was still in the wall was from the slight breathing I heard cutting into the stillness of my apartment. I made my way through the living room and turned off the TV, then fell into a deep sleep in my bed. In the morning the Wall-Person was gone. I knocked on the wall above my toilet a few times but only heard a hollow thud. I thought about calling Liz, but decided against it. I'd see her the next time she came through town. Or perhaps we'd meet in a wall, held together by plaster and wood.

Domenic Suntrapak

Domenic Suntrapak is a Fresno-based poet whose writing investigates modern landscapes. His current work focuses on regional urban identities, and how local motifs shape social behavior.

The Feat

It must be some sort of ritual.
The way the shirtless man
saunters between street corners
pumping his shoulders to and fro

and pausing, at times,
to lower his body down
onto the boiling black street-crossing
with a fluid, angular lunge.

Perhaps it is a war dance,
as he bravely dares each car
mere inches away, blurring
amid the afternoon sprawl.

Maybe it's a spell.
A complicated, somatic rite
to ward away danger
from the lay pedestrian.

Yes, while others glance
at screens, loved ones,
and the occasional newspaper,
he continues on alone

seeking the smallest
detail, and bringing the present
to heel beneath his gait.
So this is a modern ascetic.
Transfixed, I stare for some time
as the medicine man does his work
until the light grants me passage
and I exit the display with a sharp turn.

Rachel Kaufman

Rachel Kaufman is interested in memory studies, oral histories, and the ways in which literary and historical texts transmit the past. She is currently writing an archival poetry collection about New Mexico crypto-Jewish memory. Her poetry has appeared on poets.org and in *Carve Magazine, The Yale Daily News, The New Journal, Kalliope, Shibboleth,* and elsewhere. This spring, she read her poetry across the state as a winner of the 2019 Connecticut Poetry Circuit.

Reflection over Winter

The swamp across the street has been cleared and so, if you walk through the brush and bend way over, you can see your face in the water. But it is winter and windy and so your face, like the big white house, is blurry and creased. The house's flat walls look shingled, your forehead is wrinkled and small. The vulture is circling again, and when it blocks the sun and then swoops down, flashes of light reveal your reflection. The swamp is cooing, drawing you closer, drawing you in. You are wading and you look old. The branches and moss are beginning to grow back around the edges of the water. The flies are beginning to buzz again above the surface. Soon, it will all be covered, the water mostly hidden. You are unsure where you will be when this comes. The air is crisp and cold, the wind is on your neck, the sound of branches leaning over the swamp, slowly creaking and then settling, is pulsing, just barely, just there. The vultures are on the roof, spreading their wings. The sun is beginning to swallow them whole.

Richard Barnhart

Richard Barnhart kicks it hopelessly hapless, all poser kid-set space cadet sparkle sparkle, and low-key euphoria.

Hypnagogia

the moon is white phosphorous
inhaled in the smoke of her cigarette
as the hand-painted moths
wings spread iridescent
swim pools of flickering porch light

there is the familiar, though not entirely
unpleasant, tingling of slow disintegration
a softening of the skull, a loosening of the teeth
as the hand-painted moths
wings soaked in ether
swarm to envelope her

the porch light hums
she hums
the moths hum

not one remembers the words

elaine hill

---

elaine hill, a psycholinguist by training, has been a student of the cognitive shape of language and devotes her art to the possible shapes of cognition in word and form. Also a mother of two children, elaine has a penchant for answering rhetorical questions. Her work has appeared in *Contrary Magazine*, *Wide Awake*, the *Southern Journal of Linguistics*, and has won awards in South Carolina.

on explaining cigarettes to children, ages 3 and 5

it is simple. weather-gnarled
hand limps nonchalantly out
the dump truck window, flicks

lengths we cannot reach. dry,
aching mouth, twitch in the body,
the ways life drags us

onto pavement, beats us to an inch
of our lives—he can set his own fire,
wave smoke signals in the air.

habits create safety. wisps rise
to a puff, sink under his chest.
we pass the Circle K,

clouds trespass the blue-sky sun—
a black lung, dim convenience store
facade. truck rumbles on,

smoldering stick in hand,
burning into ashes, smoke
not quite reaching the sky.

Lisa Allen

Lisa Allen is pursuing an MFA in fiction at University of Massachusetts Boston. She is also a freelance journalist, writing about topics ranging from finance to science. Lisa has attended a writing residency at the Byrdcliffe Arts Colony in Woodstock, New York. She has a short story forthcoming in *Kestrel*.

The Middle Seat

6 a.m., middle seat, hopelessly awake. The man in the window seat has blinded himself with an eye mask and collared himself with a neck pillow, and he is breathing peacefully. I am angled to avoid his sleepy shoulder, too alert to sleep, too tired to work. The aisle seat woman is flipping channels on her seatback screen. I hold my right arm tight to avoid her arm. She wears glasses and a high ponytail. I can still smell the hand sanitizer she used to clean her tray table. I decide that if this kind of woman is watching TV at 6 a.m., so can I. She chooses a detective show. I glance at her screen, where a woman's body lies languid on a blue velour couch. The camera pans slowly toe-to-head, pausing on her jewelry, her diamond rings and bangle bracelets, ending on a necklace of bruises. I pick a sci-fi movie, female lead. A promising exposition of cells splitting under microscopes, inspiring bereavement, and strong supporting women.

I try to not look at the aisle seat woman's screen, but I notice when it's case closed. I miss the part about the murderer. All I see is the beat of sexual tension between the male detective and the female detective over office coffee. The woman turns off her screen and opens a book. I feel like a slacker. But on my screen, a team of women—all women!—are Going In, assault rifles strapped to their backs. It does not take long for them to find a body with a ripped-wide torso stuffed with unspooled pulsing guts. The camera probes the wet red loops of tissue and I close my eyes, swallow into nausea. When I open them, the aisle seat woman has angled her face away and pushed her book to the edge of her tray table. I consider asking if she is okay, if she wants me to turn the movie off. But she might not feel comfortable saying so, and then she would hate herself for being so polite, and it would be my fault.

The beverage cart rolls up to our row. There is no hitch in the window seat man's slow breathing. I ask for cranberry juice because it sounds cheerful, and the aisle seat woman orders a coffee. The flight attendant's blue-gloved hand pours the cranberry juice into a plastic cup and it circulates like neon blood around the knobby ice cubes, makes them crunch like toppled vertebrae.

A beast with stacked rows of jagged fangs drags one of the women in my movie down a staircase. Her head thuds on every step. I want to turn it off now, for myself. She fights the beast with her hands. This is empowering, I tell myself. The beast takes her body in its jaws and shakes her like a dog with a doll. She is still fighting. Would bailing seem anti-feminist? The aisle seat woman gets up, and I try to see her face but she looks away as she walks toward the bathroom. I tilt my head up toward the air vents. I try to imagine the sound the oxygen masks make when they eject and dangle overhead, a swarm of yellow jellyfish. My neck hurts and I find the screen again, two feet from my face. Blood slicking the floor, staining the fangs. The woman's body is still, face to the floor. It cannot get worse than this, I tell myself. Someone in corporate at the airline, someone who makes a lot of money, put this movie on the menu. Everything will get better from here. I won't say anything because we are fine. Of course we are. The worst thing anyone could do to me is ask me if I'm okay.

Ally Schwam

Ally Schwam is a poet, artist, and UX designer. Her poetry is forthcoming in *Ginosko Literary Journal* and has previously appeared in *Dream Noir, SurVision Magazine,* Tupelo Press' 30/30 Project, and others. She lives in Cambridge, Massachusetts.

Rituals // Observances

The mornings are too silent & the nights too silent.
In the summer I wash my face every hour.

I scratch foil off lottery tickets just for the feeling.
My hands look like my hands, but less capable.

In the summer I wash my face every hour.
There is an itch on my back I can't reach it I can't.

My hands look like my hands, but less capable.
I miss the birds during the winter. I miss their noise.

There is an itch on my back I can't reach it I can't.
I've been listening to heavy metal again—but louder.

I miss the birds during the winter. I miss their noise.
If you think you are dying, press your nails into your palm.

I've been listening to heavy metal again—but louder.
The mornings are too silent & the nights too silent.

If you think you are dying, press your nails into your palm.
I scratch foil off lottery tickets just for the feeling.

Eulogy

There are only three places to go on a bridge:
this way, that way, or off.

I won't choose, just let
my feet dangle.

The earth is watching me, the way
one might watch a child
as she sleeps.

Earthquakes always sing to those they bury,
remember that.

Someone said this to me, perhaps
after a funeral, after shoveling pile after pile
of dirt over the wooden casket.

I don't remember.
I don't even remember

whom the eulogy was for.

Sean William Dever

Sean William Dever is an Atlanta-based poet, educator, and editor with an MFA in Creative Writing with a focus in Poetry from Emerson College. He is a lecturer of English and Writing Studies at Clayton State University. He has recently been published or is forthcoming from *HOOT*, *Stickers*, *Unearthed Literary Magazine*, *Coffin Bell Journal*, and *Fearsome Critters Literary Magazine,* among others. Sean is the Poetry Editor of *Coffin Bell Journal* and the author of the chapbook *I've Been Cancelling Appointments with My Psychiatrist for Two Years Now,* published by Swimming with Elephants Publications.

my partner sneaks me sunshine while the doctors look away

and I pocket the little rays in my gurney
while they perform sonic echoes of my heart
and the lines rise and fall and rise and fall.

There's abnormalities banging around in my chest,
raccoons in the wall feverously knocking, then
pausing, waiting for me to catch another breath.

But my partner sings through tears, her hazel eyes
a constant throughout these tumultuous times spent
monopolizing my care from hospital to hospital around

the Greater Boston area. If Uber rides could talk
they would erupt with chimes of laughter
through failed insulin pods, windmilling, blurring together

like the irregularities the cardiologists just can't pin down.
But my partner takes my hands and draws circles in my palm;
circle after circle after circle; my partner and I in a dance,

tranced, a constant looping in an open field in rural Georgia,
against the amber sky. When these constant visits
become yearly, I take the smile she offers and memorize the lines.

Savannah Cooper

Savannah Cooper holds a BA in English—Creative Writing from Lincoln University and currently lives in Maryland with her husband and dogs. Her work has previously appeared in *Mud Season Review, Steam Ticket, Midwestern Gothic, Metonym Journal,* and *Bear Review,* among others.

Wayward

Just echoes, really, ghosts etched in ash.
The roof only half existent, a wind chime
dangling from the blackened eave.
There was something here once, a voice
that rustled in the creaking wood.
When he died, they took his eyes
and burned the rest.

He had a black dog, restless and only
half tame. For her, he left money
in a yellow envelope on the porch.
Someone took her in. Everything else
he abandoned, left scattered like buckshot.

The house was white, now charred gray.
Standing on the dusty steps, it seemed
the only structure remaining in the world,
a ragged skeleton.

Phantom

Beyond the treeline stood a darkened shape,
silver outlined, moonlight at its rough back,
eyes like embers. The stars didn't touch it,
glanced off like bullets somehow turned back.

A wolf maybe, or a mutt. A coyote
drunk on hunger and reckless need. Maybe
none of those earthly things, maybe ancient
and wild, an old god stirring from exile.

Never took a step past the trees, although
I waited. Still and unsure, a rising
panic filled the hollow space inside
my chest. I remembered no thing could walk

through walls of stone, but my rabbit heart spoke
otherwise. We were alone, us two fiends,
a wire stretched taut between. In the night,
the echo of a cry, a dying keen.

What are walls to one older than the sky,
a stark soul pacing the distant blue hills?

Paul Curtis

Paul H. Curtis lives in Brooklyn, New York. His stories have been published in *The Madison Review* and *Construction Literary Magazine*.

The Comeback

First to come back were the coyotes, but they were no use to anyone. Heidi Painter read about them in the *Post*—HOWL ABOUT THAT, said the headline—and felt vindicated. "You see?" she said to her daughter Francine. "This is what I mean about staying out of the park at night."

Francine, seated at the kitchen table, texting, did not look up. "It's not the early '90s anymore," she said. She brushed a coil of hair from her face and grimaced at her phone.

"That's unfair," said Heidi. This was a new tactic: perhaps to be heard by a teenager she needed to speak to her finely-honed sense of injustice. But Francine kept silent.

The coyotes were young males, said the *Post*. Their parents, needing room to mate again, would have kicked them out of the burrow, and so the young ones had come to the city to make it on their own. Heidi imagined sending Fran and Isaac away so that she and Scott could mate again, and she laughed, a short yip that echoed around the kitchen; Francine looked up in alarm, then went back to her phone.

Once upon a time (the *late* '90s) Heidi had leapt from her nest and landed in New York. She still considered it the boldest thing she'd ever done. And maybe it was unfair how a part of her held it against her own children that they would never make a leap like that—because after New York, where else was there to leap to? You had to sympathize with the coyotes, anyway. Even for an adaptable species, they were out of their element. But, too, they brought a touch of glamour with them: something of the actual wild had appeared in Central Park, eyes glowing in the dark heart of a city whose nocturnal aspect she had nearly forgotten.

((

The bears, though, were a bit much. The bears turned up right there in Carl Schurz Park, where one or another of the Painters would go twice a day to exercise their narcoleptic sheepdog Lenny, letting him bound around the dog run until he flopped unconscious into the dirt.

Heidi learned about the bears on a Sunday afternoon in May, just three weeks after the coyotes had made the news. She'd been out back trying to untangle a mass of sharp-leaved American bittersweet vines that were strangling her cherry tree and spawning thousands of poisonous orange berries across her little garden. Back inside, searching for better garden shears, Heidi found Isaac in the kitchen playing a game on his phone, and beside him on the counter a copy of the *Post* with the headline GRIZZLY DISCOVERY.

"The headline is misleading," said Isaac. "They're black bears. *Ursus americanus*, not *Ursus… arctos horribilis*." He sounded out the Latin carefully; it was clear he just memorized the words.

Reading the article, Heidi felt little signals pulsing up from the nerves in her arms, collecting in the hairs at the nape of her neck. "I don't want you taking Lenny to the dog run anymore," she told Isaac.

"They aren't really dangerous," Isaac said. "They're vegetarians."

Francine entered the kitchen, dressed in gym clothes. "Who are vegetarians?" she asked.

"Black bears," said Isaac.

"Why are you in gym clothes?" asked Heidi.

"There are black bears in Carl Schurz," said Isaac.

"I'm going running," said Francine. "What are bears doing in the park?"

"Waking up," said Isaac. "It's spring."

"You run?" asked Heidi.

Francine shrugged. "I felt like it."

"Mostly they eat shoots and nuts," said Isaac. "But they also eat bees."

"Bees aren't vegetables," said Francine.

"Maybe you should stick to York Avenue," said Heidi. "On your run."

"*Mostly* they're vegetarians," said Isaac.

Francine rolled her eyes. "I'm not going to be eaten by bears," she said. Heidi wished that Fran could content herself with circling the block. She worked from home partly because it afforded her, whenever she liked, the pleasure of turning up her own street. The silvery linden shade, the tree boxes guarded by laminated signs forbidding dog waste and litter, the linked townhomes with their lovingly pointed Jurassic sandstone and their long Italianate doors framed by wild acanthus leaf brackets, all one chain of affirmation: that worth continued to grow with time, that beauty was attentive to function, as fortune was to foresight, as tranquility was to the call of vigilance. But she knew better than to press the point with Francine.

Two weeks later, the bears were still there. Or, more precisely, they were back. The Parks Department had tranquilized them and delivered them to the Catskills, but they were spotted again soon after, rooting around in the shrubs near the Esplanade.

Late one evening, a few days after this sighting, Scott arrived home from work while Heidi was reading a novel on the sofa. "I saw Stan Lichtenstein," he said as he pried off his shoes and settled in next to her. "He told me he's in bear repellent now."

Heidi put her novel on the coffee table. "He's in what?"

"He's in bear repellent. He's developing a line for the urban market."

"That's ridiculous."

"I think it's brilliant. Stan's got an entrepreneurial knack."

Stan Lichtenstein had no particular knack at all, if you asked Heidi. He lost his job in finance a few years before, and since then he had flitted from project to project while his wife paid the bills. For a while he'd been talking about a wind farm on Rikers Island. And Heidi remembered how once, at the end of a dinner party, he had drunkenly described a plan to put ads on subway rats. "You know how you stand there in the station," Stan had said, gesturing, a smear of Bucheron on the elbow of his blazer, "and you just can't stop staring at the damn rats?"

"What is bear repellent?" Heidi asked.

"Well, it's just basically pepper spray. But with a picture of a bear on the package."

"Isn't pepper spray illegal?"

Scott pushed himself away from her and leaned back against the arm of the sofa. He needed a trim; the hairs at his temples were beginning to outpace the stragglers at the top of his head. There was a hole in one of his socks, at the ball of the foot. He was usually so careful to be rid of socks with holes. They reminded him of his own mortality.

The point, he said, was that you had to admire how Stan was getting mileage out of this whole bear thing. It wasn't just Carl Schurz anymore. There were bears on the West Side, downtown, in Prospect Park. One had turned up inside a token booth at Queens Plaza. There was a market here, and Stan was taking advantage.

One key to a successful marriage, Heidi had determined, was the mutual suspension of disbelief. The labor of loving another—not just for now but over the long term—involved a willingness to work at maintaining an unredeemed faith in one's partner, to hear his aimless fantasies and complaints with the same respect you'd given him all those years ago, when he leaned into you at Bamonte's and spoke with so much fervor about all that you both believed was yet to come. Heidi chose to change the subject. "Did you know that our daughter has taken up jogging?"

Scott said nothing for a moment, and then he nodded. "Good for her," he said. "Physical fitness." And he lay back and closed his eyes and seemed to daydream for a while, and before very long he was snoring.

⟨

It was with the comeback of the beavers that things really began to change. They made a dramatic arrival: one morning in July, the Harlem River was sent up over its banks by a massive dam which seemed to have been constructed overnight. The waters flooded Yankee Stadium and forced the cancellation of a doubleheader. DAM YANKEES, said the covers of both the *Post* and the *Daily News*.

The following Friday, Scott turned up in the kitchen only an hour after he left for work. A line of poplars had sprung up along Second Avenue, fouling the traffic, and the motionless cars had been overtaken by an enormous herd of deer. Sitting in the idle taxi, watching chestnut-colored fur stream by, white tails flashing behind, Scott had come to a decision.

"Beaver pelts," he said.

Hadn't there been a time when she thrilled at any unexpected chance to see him? Now she kept her eyes on her computer, half-listening, in the manner of an Isaac or a Fran. Scott complained about work for a while, and she heard him say "beaver pelts," but it was only when he said "Stan Lichtenstein" that she turned to him with her attention undivided.

"You want to do *what* with Stan Lichtenstein?"

"We buy them off the trappers for a few bucks a unit, hire people to do the processing, and then we move the furs at a pretty good markup."

"Processing?" asked Francine. She was sitting in a chair, applying polish to the toenails on her dirty foot. Isaac dangled from a stool, jiggling his leg. His toes nearly reached the floor. They hadn't done that before.

"Skinning them," said Isaac. "Right, Dad? And then you soak them in vinegar."

"Gross," said Francine.

"Something like that," said Scott. "But we're just the middlemen."

"Please go back," said Heidi. "You want us to quit our jobs—"

"Vinegar and slaked lime," said Isaac. He was reading from a website on his phone. "And alum. What's that?"

"—and go into business with Stan Lichtenstein—"

"Selling furs to the European market."

"The what market?"

"They make hats," said Scott. "And coats."

Francine leaned in to blow on her toes. "You're going to make coats?" she asked.

"We're just the middlemen," Scott said again.

It hit him in the cab: the law was not good business anymore. If the profit of law was found in the gap between behavior and expectations, what good was litigation now that no one could know what to expect? Now that all the laws were being unwound?

Heidi could not believe that they were talking about this. "How much of our life savings are you wanting to sink into this Stan Lichtenstein scheme?"

"Alum," Isaac read. "Hydrated potassium aluminum sulfate."

"It's my scheme as much as his," said Scott. "Our scheme, I mean. It could be. Yours and mine." His eyes were wet, the way they used to get whenever he said something especially sincere. He always claimed to hate how they did that. Heidi hadn't hated it.

"Times are changing," said Scott. "We need to adapt."

How was she supposed to react to a proposal like this one? What to do when the fervor returned?

"I thought Stan was in bear repellent," Heidi said.

"FDA problems," said Scott. "It's hard to get people to understand that it isn't like mosquito repellent. You're not supposed to spray it on yourself."

"People are stupid," said Isaac.

"True," said Francine. "People are."

"But this is different," said Scott. "This is better. I can almost guarantee you that this will not go wrong."

The most comforting thing about faith, in truth, was that it was so rarely redeemed. As time ran away from you, as your children leapt from the bassinet to high school in an interval so small it could hardly have contained a season of the years you spent in college, your faith—in the world and in yourself and in your partner—expired slowly over the whole long sweep of things. Having once been wound tight, it lost momentum by degrees, almost imperceptibly. It was the Great Slackening, the easing of a system of expectation whose logic otherwise carried you relentlessly toward a confrontation with your own unsatisfying obituary. It was a kind of happiness, Heidi thought. Why risk it for a reset?

"I'm not asking you to say yes," said Scott. "Not yet. Just not no."

The nakedness in his voice: she remembered it from Bamonte's. She remembered the tickle of his words in her ear, the linguine she'd been too excited to finish. She thought that it wasn't a matter of mechanics after all; it wasn't a question of resetting or rewinding. She sensed that perhaps this risk *wanted* to be taken, that the risk was something animate and untamed but devoted to her, something that had stuck near to her for years, waiting for her to embrace it. She felt this notion in her scalp, radiating heat.

Her answer was not yes—not yet. But it was not no.

《

The American bittersweet disappeared. Or it didn't disappear, so much as it was overwhelmed. The garden itself was absorbed into a thickening jungle that broke down the fences between the back lots; it grew up and over the brownstones and onto the sidewalks and into the streets. It was beyond cultivation: Heidi only sought to identify what she could. There was sweet flag, wild indigo, snakeroot, and jewelweed; there was columbine and bearberry and maidenhair fern; there was wakerobin and beach plum and Virginia creeper; there was white milkweed in supernova clusters orbited by butterflies. Maple saplings stretched toward adolescence. One morning, she found an orchid on her stoop.

It was a good year. The European market proved insatiable for beaver pelts, and Painter & Lichtenstein LLC, while highly leveraged, was moving units at a remarkable pace. Scott was as happy as she'd ever seen him, though she didn't see much of him. He handled sales while Heidi managed operations. It was endless work: bargaining with the fractious multitudes of free-agent trappers, smoothing over labor troubles at the tannery, maintaining quality control, keeping up with ever-increasing shipping costs. Stan Lichtenstein's role in the concern was never quite clear, but it didn't matter much. For all the labor involved, there was no question that they had made the right move. Business boomed; the money rolled in; the Painters prospered.

There was little time to spend together as a family, but everyone seemed happy. Francine gave up jogging and took up watercolors and gave up watercolors and took up archery; a passel of girls from her school followed her dutifully into each new hobby. She said she wanted to apply to Sarah Lawrence. Isaac amassed a fortune in digital equipment of some sort and told his parents he was setting the human genome to music. Meanwhile, the *Law Journal* reported that what remained of Scott's old firm had been swallowed up in a contentious merger which had involved one obstructionist partner being thrown, literally, to the wolves.

There were so many less fortunate families. Heidi saw them on television: families less able to adapt to all the changes in the world. Families losing their homes and their livelihoods. Families falling apart. The Painters were fortunate enough to be able to help. They wrote a lot of checks. They were able to help because Scott had been right, and Heidi had been right to trust him.

It was Francine who first alerted them to the trouble.

They were eating in the dining room: the formal Sunday dinner Heidi had began to insist upon once she realized that it was the only time the four of them were ever likely to be in the same room together. It was one year and five months from the day she had first read about the coyotes. Leaning over to pluck a candied pear from a serving tray with her fork, Francine said, "Doesn't it seem like there are too many beavers?"

The question struck Heidi as absurd, and she laughed, and it felt good to be at the dining room table with her family, laughing, but she saw how Scott went pale and she began to understand.

"Do you think?" asked Scott.

Francine shrugged. "I don't know. I just mean no matter how many you skin, there seem to be twice as many showing up every month."

Isaac agreed. At West Point, he noted, the dam had to be blown up almost every other day now. Newburgh was near-unlivable with all the flooding.

This should be a funny conversation, thought Heidi. Too many beavers should be funny! "How can there be too many beavers?" she asked, but she could hear the panic in her own laughter.

Scott was silent.

"No, it's good, I guess," said Francine. "More for everybody. Kylie Johanssen's family's getting into beaver pelts now."

"Are they?" asked Scott.

"*Everybody's* getting into beaver pelts now," said Francine.

It happened only days later. THE DAM BREAKS, reported the *Post*. BEAVER BUBBLE BURSTS, said the *Daily News*. How could they not have seen it coming? Or had they seen it coming but chosen to ignore it, and if so, how could they have ignored it? They had everything invested in beaver pelts, which now traded for pennies on the dollar against their previous price. They followed their dreams, but so had everyone else, and now nobody's dreams were worth anything.

Scott gathered the family in extraordinary session on a Thursday afternoon. "I've ruined us," he said.

Heidi was prepared for this. "First of all," she said, "we did this, together. And second, we're never ruined. There's always something else."

Scott's voice was shrunken by despair. "What else?" he asked.

"For instance," said Heidi, "the oysters have come back."

((

Moving to Brooklyn was hardest for Francine. Scott was too traumatized to react much, at first, and Isaac handled the loss of his bedroom and his digital machinery with surprising equanimity—he invested his last cash in a ten-year-old hardbound encyclopedia set, and fell mutteringly into its volumes whenever he had an opportunity. For Heidi, the move was another adventure, a chance to explore new territory, to clear a new garden and grow corn and beans and squash, to affirm that her life hadn't ended with her arrival on, or her departure from, the Upper East Side.

The world was now a procession of lasts: the last broadcast, the last flight, the last flicker of electricity, the last day of school forever. The lasts all ran in one direction, but only if you looked at them that way; if you looked at them another way, each last gave onto a next. The bank, for instance, had outlasted the last of the Painters' savings, surviving long enough to take their brownstone away, but Heidi had the satisfaction of knowing that within a few years the new owners would find their asset pulled to pieces by the roots and vines that had already begun to invade its interior. Change, she found, was not necessarily a matter of blown expectations. Brooklyn wasn't worse than the Upper East Side. It was just next.

But Francine struggled to adjust. Phoneless and adrift in an outer borough, crowded with her family into one of the oystermen's shacks along the water's edge in Bay Ridge, without hope of ever making it to Sarah Lawrence, she alternated between bouts of depression and acts of rebellion. She wished she had a *normal* family, she said, impervious to the argument that there *were* no normal families anymore, at least not by her definition. The worst point came when she managed to set fire to the rowboat that represented the only real capital the Painters had left; she claimed it was accidental, but this was plainly a lie.

"That's it for us," Scott said, slumping into a chair beside the woodstove. "We'll be wading around in the mud now."

And that was what they did. Each morning at dawn, the four Painters put on their boots and picked up their rakes and squished through the muck, combing bivalves into piles, and in the afternoons they gathered up the piles and Scott and Fran took most of them to market in a wheelbarrow while Heidi and Isaac shucked the rest and put them on ice with lemon wedges and sold them at the Painter's Fine Oysters booth beneath the abandoned expressway on Third Avenue. At the sorting table, Francine would lay out her catch with sullen eyes, silent because her lips were cold, and because, Heidi presumed, she could not give expression to the mixture of anger and shame she felt. Scott, too, would offer his catch in silence, but it was an eager silence, a prayer for Heidi's approval. Each oyster Scott and Francine contributed was a token of restitution, and it took some time for them to understand that what Heidi sought, what the family needed, was not restitution, but trust.

As they came to understand this, they began to change. Francine emerged from her silence and in time developed a genuine enthusiasm for oystering; Heidi was impressed by the alacrity with which she pushed through unpredictable currents, dodging urchins and anemones and often bringing in the biggest haul. One cold blue morning Heidi watched Francine, up to her knees in the brackish water, work open an oyster with her knife and pull out a tiny pearl, which she held in her blue fingers and examined rapturously, and Heidi thought that even with the mud on her face and in her hair she looked lovely; and Isaac said that the pearl was worthless, that these were *Crassostrea virginica*, not pearl oysters, but Francine only laughed and said she didn't care, that it was a New York pearl, and it was perfect.

The oysters multiplied endlessly throughout the city's waterways, spats making beds from Jamaica Bay to the Bronx, fueling the biggest oyster boom New York had seen in centuries. The Painters profited enough for a couple of years to afford a decent life in their cozy Bay Ridge hut, which seemed to smell permanently of wet sheepdog, but never really enough to get ahead. Which wasn't to say that getting ahead meant anything anymore. All in all, Heidi thought, they were doing pretty well.

⟨

Heidi made this point to Scott one winter evening about two years after the oyster boom, as they sat, arms linked, beside their campfire. "All in all," she said, "we're doing pretty well."

"We are," said Scott. Wild gray hair at his temples; perfectly bald on top. But lean, in the way he'd been a very long time ago.

"Considering everything."

"Considering everything," said Scott.

They were in the Bronx—Heidi figured it for Morris Park—tracking a herd of mastodons. Dinner fires tended by the other families in their band lay smoke across the campsite; through the dusk and the haze they could see Isaac standing patiently atop a snow bank beside the slumped silhouette of Lenny.

"Do you remember when you proposed to me?" asked Heidi.

Scott nodded. "At Bamonte's," he said. "Over linguine." He fed a yellowed copy of the *Post* into the fire, then reached to turn the rabbit. It occurred to Heidi that once they caught the mastodon they would need a bigger spit.

"I suppose it's gone now," she said.

"Bamonte's? I suppose it is."

"I have to say," said Heidi, "I'm impressed with us."

Scott tore a chunk of flesh from the rabbit and bit down to test it. "Mm," he said in agreement. "Also, I was thinking."

"I mean, here we are."

"Here we are," said Scott. "Also, I was thinking we should do something for Isaac. Some sort of coming-of-age type thing."

"I think he already came of age," said Heidi. "He's seventeen."

"I just mean, since college isn't an option," said Scott.

"We didn't do anything for Fran."

"But she has her own band now. I'm just thinking coming-of-age, leaving the nest, you know."

"A ceremony?"

"Why not?"

"Drink the blood of a deer? Go on a spirit quest?" She was joking, but it didn't mean she disagreed.

"I don't know. Something like that."

It was true that without some sort of intervention Isaac was unlikely to seek his own fortune any time soon. He was as uncomplaining as ever, but as his resources had dwindled he seemed to have retreated deeper into his own mind. He still carried a single mildewed volume of his old encyclopedia—Ma-Mn—and he dug into it so often that Heidi was sure he memorized it. But did that mean he was unhappy? Did that mean he needed to be pushed? It wasn't so clear.

"We can make it up as we go along," said Scott.

"We can," said Heidi.

She was looking forward to the spring. There would be strawberries and birdsong and wildflowers, and she could clear a new garden somewhere pleasant, and Francine and her band would come back from their winter caribou grounds in New Jersey, and they could have family dinners and talk about life and the world and whatever else. It would be nice.

A wind lifted the smoke from the campsite and carried the sound of laughter from the Lichtenstein tent, and Isaac came back with Lenny in tow, and Scott took the rabbit from the fire, and they ate.

☾

Eventually the glaciers came back. A great wall of ice rolled down from the north, obliterating Sarah Lawrence and Newburgh and Morris Park and Queens Plaza and Carl Schurz and Bay Ridge, crushing New York City into gravel and sand, and sealing it away beneath a quarter mile of silence, which held for almost a thousand years. And then, inch by inch, the glaciers rolled away again, melting day by day and leaving new inches of bare earth behind them each day.

Don Thompson

Don Thompson has been writing about the San Joaquin Valley for over fifty years, including a dozen or so books and chapbooks. For more info and links to publishers, visit his website at www.don-e-thompson.com.

Mesquite

Only a shrub, beneath notice,
this shabby genteel mesquite
sustains its delusional status
as a tree.

The last tatters of its foliage
cling like velvet well into decline
from green to gray
to gone.

You can see its bones, arthritic,
but not that taproot sinking
almost deeper than death
can reach.

Emily Hoover

Emily Hoover is a poet, fiction writer, and book reviewer based in Las Vegas. Her fiction has most recently appeared in *BULL* and *Gravel*, and her poems have been featured in *Potluck Magazine*, *FIVE:2:ONE*, and *the tiny journal*. Emily's book reviews have been published by *The Los Angeles Review*, *Necessary Fiction*, *Ploughshares* blog, *The Collagist*, and others. She is a lecturer of English at Nevada State College.

Arguing with You on the Phone in the McDonald's Parking Lot off I-17

No one remembers

the smell of autumn: dead leaves

& petrified joy.

Elevation Stillness

Shadows of midday light, cast from pine trees
above, envelop us. Still, we are mute.
Golden. Warm. Motionless because of these
unseen stars, slight breezes, bare arms, acute
sense of presence. Breathing. Your eyes open—
you hold me in your gaze; I am small
against the rock face. I am unbroken,
but not without jagged edges. A squall
that has left denim faded, coffee stains.
You know I can see our mountains from here.
I'll remember this each time the moon wanes,
waxes, eclipses. Covered in clouds, we're
constant: one body now, one heart, one lung.
It's quiet before howling of the young.

M. Pavan Clark

M. Pavan Clark is a queer Southern writer whose work appears in *Apalachee Review, Cream City Review, Ontario Review, Sinister Wisdom, Impossible Archetype, Pilgrimage,* and elsewhere, and is forthcoming in *Foglifter, Loch Raven Review, Pangyrus, Pomme Journal, Qwerty,* and *Shenandoah,* among others. *Best American Essays 2011* recognized her creative nonfiction among the Notable Essays, and her work is a 2019 Best of the Net nominee. She lives in the Southwest. Her name rhymes with raven.

How to Prepare for a Visit from the Woman
Who Is Not Your Lover

Clean the house, but not too clean. Sweep and vacuum, wash dishes, and do laundry. Change the sheets on the guest bed, smooth the quilt, plump the pillows, dust the dresser. Get on your knees and scrub the bathtub. She will have been traveling two days by train in coach. She deserves a sparkling tub and fresh towels in her favorite color. Straighten your books and papers and remove them from the dining room table. Don't do more. The clutter must be familiar.

Stock up on organic fruits and vegetables, tofu, soymilk, and tea. Do not buy flowers for the dining room table. She will know they are not for the dining room table. Arrange the fruit in a pretty bowl and make that a centerpiece.

Shower. Then clean the tub again. Allow time for your hair to dry so you can check it before she sees you. Ideally it should look full and shaggy, devil-may-care, as though you weren't trying. It should shine in the sun and smell good when she hugs you hello.

Consider your essential oils. Do you wish to smell like spruce with hints of clove and citrus, or tobacco and leather, or maybe myrrh? Screw the caps back on. Let soap be scent enough. You rarely wear perfume so early in the day. She will know you made the effort just for her, and you do not wish to give yourself away.

As for what to wear, look good, but not your best. Tempting as it is, do not wear red and black. She dreams of you in red and black. Do not put on the black leather jacket she dreamed you were wearing. It's too warm, anyway. Choose the new blue jeans; they grip your ass and thighs, but aren't too tight. Add a plain white T and a denim shirt, unbuttoned and untucked. You will look like your regular self. You will look as good as you can without really trying. She won't know you tried. It is most important that she not know you tried.

Do not wash the car. Do not vacuum the dog fur and dirt you've tracked in these past months. Do remove the scattered papers and receipts, tangled earbuds, and empty water bottle from the passenger seat. Do no more.

Check the train schedule repeatedly. For once, it's running on time.

In the car, do not put on the playlist you made to think of her. The album *Knife* by Aztec Camera seems a safe choice, but don't listen closely. Some lyrics divine your future. Ever after, you will hear their stichomancy and think of her.

Before backing down the driveway, text to say you'll be there when the train pulls in. Drive with the window down. Bask in this beautiful autumn day. While it is inadvisable to read her reply, do it anyway, at a stoplight. It will say, "I'm already here." When the light turns green, do not speed. It is inadvisable to call while driving, but do it anyway. You will curse, and she will laugh and say, "Take your time." The lanes ahead are blocked and traffic is backed up, so curse again, but only in fun. Tell her you'll see her soon. Hang up. Do not speed. Do not weave or tailgate. Twenty minutes will crawl by.

When you pull up at the train station and spot her, park sensibly. Leave space for other drivers. It's okay to greet her with your biggest smile. You always do. She stands with her baggage at her feet and a small animal in her arms. Its head weaves on its slender neck, tracing figure eights. A stray, no doubt—it happens all the time. She found a box turtle on her last visit—and years ago, a ferret. This looks like a ferret, but as you draw near, you see it's the puppet she told you about, the feathered green dragon she designed and sculpted. Marvel: "It's alive!" Take care to hug her without crushing the dragon. There's time later for a proper hug. Take one of her bags. She will say it's heavy and she can carry it herself. Remind her she has traveled a long way to be with you. Say it's the least you can do.

In the car, ask if she'd rather get a bite to eat or go home. It is important to be considerate. She has been traveling by coach for two days. She will choose home. As you drive, keep your eyes on the road. Answer her questions about the music. Do not look too long at her silvery eyes, her beguiling smile, or the fabulous dragon craning its neck and stretching its wings. She is precious cargo. Drive accordingly.

Inside the house, she will unload her baggage and lay down the dragon and give you a proper hug. She will hold you close, much closer than ever before. Show no surprise. Respond in kind. Enjoy the fit of her body, its curves and contours. Think of her body only in terms of contours. Then, what the hell, go ahead: think of her breasts as breasts, savor how good they feel full and soft and delectable against your ribcage, relish the flare and tilt of her hips. Promise yourself you won't let go until she lets go.

When she doesn't let go, quick, improvise! There is no way to prepare for this.

Afterward, long afterward, she will take the blame for making the first move. Repeatedly she will take the blame. She will steep herself in shame. Remember your manners. Remind her you seized opportunity, you welcomed her whole.

Daniel Edward Moore

Daniel Edward Moore lives in Washington on Whidbey Island with the poet, Laura Coe Moore. His poems have been in *Spoon River Poetry Review, Columbia Journal, Cream City Review, Western Humanities Review, phoebe, Mid-American Review, december,* and others. His poems are forthcoming in *Weber Review, West Trade Review, Duende Literary Journal, Isthmus Review, The Meadow, Bluestem Magazine, Faultline Journal of Arts & Letters, Slipstream,* and *Timber.* His chapbook *Boys* is forthcoming from Duck Lake Books (February 2020). He was a finalist of the Brick Road Poetry Prize for *Waxing the Dents* (April 2020). His work has been nominated for Pushcart Prizes and Best of the Net. Visit him at Danieledwardmoore.com.

Always Never Enough

Always is never enough
                       & never enough
       always makes you
question the meaning   of everything present

beyond the chance of you
                   going away beyond
    the chance of you not
coming home   not finding your keys

not brushing your teeth
                 not kissing the kids
    goodnight as they sleep
dreaming of you   being   always there

that kind of never enough
               little breastbone
    breaking apart in a
stranger's hand   crawling from the cave

of a white lab coat
             tied to your heart with
    a stethoscope counting
the never enough   beats of you

now only a thought
             lasting long enough
    for someone to say
what they always knew   & you will never hear.

Res Northcraft

Res Northcraft studies English Literature at the University of Toledo. Their writing won the 2018 and 2019 Shapiro Awards, and their poetry has appeared in *Khroma*, *The Mill*, and *The Rectangle*. A native of Pittsburgh, Pennsylvania, they enjoy working in childcare services for the military abroad.

pull the thin-heat over moon-flesh & let the bursting go.

—your
grandmother

said she would be there

like she really thought

she could be, her words

dripping like
merlot from the plastic
cup & the drunk

gnat's mosquito-belly
turned soft & a pinprick
of black legs

bent toward some middle, some fibonacci center, something cosmic & paisley
& so much bigger than your green

eyes.   pull the body out.
when water   turns brown, for a moment we all pray, despite

the feathers
gray-turned, falling
limp from the sky—

Amy Lauren

Amy Lauren was a finalist for the 2019 Tennessee Williams Poetry Prize. Her chapbooks include *Prodigal*, *God With Us*, and *She/Her/Hers*. Her poems have appeared in publications such as *The Gay & Lesbian Review* with four Pushcart Prize nominations. A graduate of Mississippi College, she currently lives in Florida with her wife.

Straight, Narrow

Moss wreaths wrought his path
rotting with old wood, abandoned
signpost's arms pointing to   nowhere cypresses can tell.

Needles adorn shorelines
nailed with planks.   This is
the spot where Papa saw
Jesus. Right there.   Right

where branches bow
under the eagle's nest,   a holy weight.
Lightning crashed, he dropped
his oar, helds up his   hands

just to let rain soak   his skin.
A red wolf howled
so he jumped back
and paddled here real   quick

to tell me. Yes, it was   Jesus
floating creekside, flaming
sword real as dragonflies,
pickerelweeds aglow and   crowning

his head in dead night.   Stretched
forth algae hands to grab
your Papa's collar, shake   sin
right out of him. So that's

where he's gone tonight,
retracing the narrow to find his savior.
Don't call, he's got to focus
on footprints, draw a map,   taste

every dewberry on the narrow.
Don't laugh, if we could too   haunt
that healing hem, we'd be
back desperate for one more   embrace

from those holy arms.

Cal Setar

Cal Setar is a writer living in Philadelphia. Previously, his work has appeared in *The Woven Tale Press, Solstice Literary Magazine,* and elsewhere. He is more than he is now, he swears.

The Most Famous Man in Philadelphia

It was almost as if he appeared out of nowhere, materializing in the chill air of the station, one second looking beyond me, over my shoulder as the board flips and the times and tracks update, the next laughing and pointing and grinning at me with bright white teeth, calling me a *ham* and thanking me for saving his spot, his spot, his *spot*.

How comfortable, how at home he looks; it was as if he'd always been there, I think, had maybe never *not* been there. But somehow, in my hurry, I just never noticed.

He sits and eyes me, some kind of mischievous writ wild and winking on his face and, already annoyed, already bothered, already ready for this strange episode to be over and done with, I busy myself with my phone, my hands, my legs, the floor, with looking at anything and everything and seeing nothing, with practicing the not-so-ancient art of seeing without comprehending, existing without being.

Still, I see him there, see him smiling and pointing and wait—what's this? He's pulling out a pad of paper now, whisking it from some unknown and unseen fold near his heart, his large, wrinkled hand suddenly full of taped-up pencils and something that looks like a marker but might not be, glancing down and glancing up and glancing down and glancing up, seemingly studying me, me in my obvious disinterest, me in my unhappy discomfort, me in my wish to be left alone and how far could the bathrooms really be and why the hell wasn't she back yet? Maybe I need a pretzel, I think. Or a water bottle. A coffee or a tea or a nice long walk along every column, every door, every inch of the four great walls of this place.

When I finally look up, he smiles all over again, smiles as if he'd been waiting for me and only me, always me, never not me, all this time.

"You *ham*. Oh, look at *you*. You *ham*… you're a pretty boy, ain't you? That's what I'm gonna call you. Pretty Boy. Well, Pretty Boy Number Two. I'm Pretty Boy Number One, ya know."

His eyes go wide and white as his teeth as he dissolves into a fit of laughter that has to be forced, I think, but somehow doesn't feel it, doesn't tug at my ear the way make-believe usually does, trying to force its way in without actual fit or feeling.

But then, just like that, he's serious, intensely serious, glancing down and glancing up and glancing down and glancing up and asking me to smile now, that's it, gimme that smile, you really are a Pretty Boy, aren't you? you little Pretty Boy, you little *ham*, all the while moving the pencil over the page, stopping and starting and sketching without looking, sketching without lifting the arm of his oversized leather jacket, perfunctorily peering down at his work over the tops of the glasses perched on the tip of his nose, lifting them to look at me through clouded lenses, smiling and laughing and drawing, drawing, drawing me in until I can't stand it anymore and I crane my neck to see and he lifts the pad away with a flourish, cackling and wide-eyed as ever.

"Look at *you*! Look at you wantin' to see! Oh, Pretty Boy—Pretty Boy Number Two, I should say. You really are somethin' else. You character you. You— you... *ham*!"

He cackles again, the sound seeming to expand outward, trying desperately to fill the station and nearly succeeding before narrowing down and darting into me, bouncing through the hollows of my head, leaving behind a ringing that fades only when I realize he's next to me on my bench now, leaned comfortably against the hard edges of the wood, pad propped on a crossed knee— just high enough that I still can't see—glancing down and glancing up, sketching and swiping with the back of his hand and using something that looks like a pencil but isn't to erase or maybe smudge and then sketching again, smiling with those big white teeth and those wide white eyes, muttering about something or other, this or that, ham, ham, *ham*, all the while sketching, always sketching, never not sketching.

"I'm famous, you know."

He's holding something out to me; a bird or a badge, a body of some kind, something off-white and fluttering, something I eventually recognize as a laminated piece of paper, the corners peeling, the plastic marked and scuffed and the printed words faded almost to the point of illegibility. I can see there's a picture of a local landmark on it. I take it without meaning to, doing as he says without any conscious intent; read both sides, Pretty Boy Number Two, you character, you *ham*.

I tell myself the truth.

I tell myself it *must* be the truth.

I tell myself the truth is bald and boring and uglier than any of us would like to admit. That truth and make-believe may live inside the same station, but follow separate tracks. That they simply cannot, would not, will not occupy the same track.

I tell myself it must be true.

He's a normal man, just a normal man in an oversized leather jacket, sick and hungry and tired, probably looking for drugs or drink or something darker, probably buttering me up for the final plunge, the final flourish, probably drawing stick figures while he fishes in my coat pocket for my wallet or my phone or my senses.

I hug my bag, sitting on the bench between us, closer.

Oh, I think, willing myself back to the chill air and the hard edges and the real, the real, the *real*.

I've seen this show before, I think.

You couldn't make it more than a month in the city without some panhandler or sopping drunk handing you a card or a pack of tissues or an empty hat, dirty pennies still stuck to the dingy fabric at the bottom. And it might not come right away, if you were lucky—or, in this case, not-so-lucky—it might disguise itself, making practical use of your disgust, your discomfort, remaining hidden behind a handful of hard smiles or exaggerated silences, the sorriest story you ever did hear hummed out in hushed tones over the low vibration of a passing bus, an arriving subway train. But eventually the hook came, always came, because it was always there, had always been there, would always be there, hidden in the choicest section of the thickest piece, just waiting to pull tight and drag you down to exasperation. To annoyance. Anger, even. To, just take it. Just take it and go. Leave me to my life and my living, leave me to my happiness and my home, my free and my easy, right back to seeing without comprehending, right back to existing without being.

That's all this is, I think. A show. Waiting to start.

Waiting for me. Or someone like me. Someone just like me, but not *me*, not me specifically, of course not me, not me, not *me*. That'd be crazy. That'd be wild.

That'd be make-believe.

I feel cheated somehow.

Soiled. This thing—this strange, not-at-all-strange thing unfolding in front of me, this weird little exchange we've been sharing in the high-ceilinged emptiness of the station—already turned from bright, blinding white to brown and cracked and broken.

He didn't materialize out of thin air, I realize, but he *had* always been there.

Still, I read. Still, I go where it is he wants to take me.

He is homeless. Well, he *was* homeless. Used to take his pad and pencils to that local landmark and draw people's portraits for money. Apparently, he drew the picture of whoever wrote the article I was reading, the one he'd probably went to great lengths to have printed and laminated so he could take it around with him, slipping it into people—his subjects', his marks', his *characters'*—unsuspecting hands.

The guy liked the way he'd drawn his beard. The guy who'd written the article; he liked the way his beard looked in the portrait.

And there, just there, scrawled in an awkward, blocky hand at the bottom right of the image depicting what he'd drawn that fateful day, a name.

"Hi, Irving."

He recoils, eyes gone wide all over again.

"See! I told you, Pretty Boy! I told you… well. Pretty Boy Number Two! I'm *famous*. Famous as they come. I used to be homeless, but I'm not anymore. Nope, nope, *nope*. I'm famous now. Famous, and not homeless. Not at all. Nope."

He leans in, a gnarled hand appearing on my shoulder, pulling me toward him as his face hovers nearer and nearer to mine. He's serious again, the eyes over the tops of his glasses happy, but hard.

"When I was homeless, I'd do my portraits for money. But I ain't gotta do that now. Now, I do it for everyone else. To give back to the rest of the city's homeless. I do it so they can get something to eat. A place to stay. Something warm to wear. For them, for them, for *them*."

I nod, feeling the hook pull tight as he dissolves in another fit of unforced laughter.

I risk a peek, trying once more to get a glimpse of what he'd drawn, thinking of the thin lines of the tiny drawing on the laminated article, but he sees and snatches it away before I can.

"Oh, Pretty *Boy*! Look at you! You character! You *ham*! You wanna see, don't you? Yeah, you wanna see. Pretty Boy. Pretty Boy Number Two. Número dos.

I'm Number One now, and don't you forget it! Don't you forget it! You wanna see. I know you wanna see."

A sly smile and he's tugging on the shoulder of my jacket, rocking back and forth like a little kid thinking of the funniest thing he'd ever seen, barely able to contain all the laughter wanting to spill up and out and onto the floor.

"You wanna see, don't you? Oh, Pretty *Boy*. Oh, Pretty Boy. I know you want to. I know. Number Two. That's you. That's you, Pretty Boy. That's *you*."

A nod and a wink and he's back to his drawing, looking me up and down, telling me to hold myself in that position, no not that one, Pretty Boy, keep your head straight, look at me, oh, you character, you *ham*, okay, now smile, smile big and wide, oh, you're not much for smiling, eh? that's fine, that's fine, that's *just* fine, we can work around that, do you know why I draw men, Pretty Boy? do you know why I draw men and not women? it's because we're not so pretty, well, most of us aren't anyway, not like you, Pretty Boy, not like you, *Number Two*, but it's because we're not so pretty and what's the point in trying to draw something that's already as beautiful as it ever could be? Huh? Didja ever think of that one, Pretty Boy? Huh? *Huh*?

And he's serious again, adding little flourishes here and there, smudging something or another, the pad held at an angle just severe enough that I still can't see what it is he's drawing, only now, I realize, he's not calling me Pretty Boy, not calling me a character or a *ham*, not laughing and pointing and grabbing at my coat. He's serious in a whole new way, looking down at me over the tops of his glasses and asking me a question, a question, a *question*. What doesn't, at first, seem a strange question, an uncomfortable query, but that irks me just the same, the fit as awkward and ill-fitting as his laughter somehow hadn't been.

"Have you ever been homeless?"

No.

No, I say. I've never been homeless.

He nods, sniffs, settles back. Tells me the story again. *His* story. The story written out on the laminated paper by a man who liked the way he—the way *Irving*—had drawn him. I start to tell him I know the story already, I know the story already and my girlfriend should be coming back from the bathroom soon and I should go and check the trains, check the times, see what track I'm meant to queue up at, but he's staring at me over his dollar store glasses, talking in low tones of his life on the street, of showing up at the local landmark to draw people and ask them for something, just a little something in exchange, and it's like I'm stuck, like I can't move, like I have no choice but to sit and listen while this man sinks the hook into the soft flesh of my cheek, working whatever magic he could muster on me, and even as I'm reaching for my wallet, pursing my lips like you got me, you caught me, hook, line, and sinker, even as I'm pulling out a handful of ones, he's still talking, still telling me about his work now, about the city's homeless, the need, the need, *their* need, and I'm thinking, even now I'm thinking, yeah right, yeah right, thinking we're not talking about anyone's need but *yours*, old man, *your* need, booze or drugs or food or whatever else it could be, and I'm pushing the money into his hands like I'm trying to shoo away a troubling thought but he's leaned back, face filled with shock at the sight of the wilted green, the not-dying-but-long-dead bouquet I tried to force on him, a hand to his chest like he might faint from fright.

Now, I'm thinking, how smart. How cagey. Catch people from out of town as they're about to hop on a train out of the city, tempt them with a picture, a portrait, a keepsake, something they'll get to remember forever, even if the picture itself is lost in time, in due time, as all things are inevitably lost, and then tell them they'll be helping the city's homeless to boot.

And if all else fails? Guilt can move mountains, if applied correctly.

"You ever been homeless?"

Like his eyes, there's no softness this time, no chiding, no good-natured ribbing, no Pretty Boy—actually, Pretty Boy Number Two—no you character, you *ham*, no oh well, no I've seen what you wouldn't believe, but I'm here now, still here, still here after all and everything so what's the use of doing anything but laugh, laugh at all of it, at every last thing, even you?

He's really asking. I see that now.

Again, I say no. I even shake my head, looking around at the station as I do, wishing Alley would hurry up, wishing she'd come back from the bathroom already to interrupt and pull me away, to do what I seemingly couldn't do on my own. But she's nowhere and I'm stuck, meeting Irving's cold gaze and saying no, I've never been homeless, looking from him to the dollars in my extended hand and thinking what a cheap son of a bitch, what a cheap, cheap son of a bitch.

"What do you think three dollars can buy you on the street? What do you think that's going to get the city's homeless? I can't give you the portrait for three dollars, Pretty Boy. No way, nuh-uh. That's nothing, son. That's nothing. Can't even buy some french fries. Not french fries, not a sandwich, not a good night's sleep, not a coat or even a gosh darn coffee. I couldn't get a foot massage from a soldering iron, even if I wanted to."

He lifts the cuff of his crossed leg, rapping a knob of knuckle against the metal where his left foot used to be, pursing his lips at the sad, sad green, still sweating in my hand.

The hard sell, I think, the full press, pity for pay, but even as I'm thinking it, even as I'm sheepishly pulling my hand back—not all the way, but far enough that it looks like I might just be clutching the money at my hip—it feels mean, feels wrong. It's right, I know it is because I've seen this show before, because you don't just paint a picture—of a life or a person—unless you mean to show it to someone.

He wants more. Of course, he wants more. Who, I think, doesn't?

I comfort myself with the knowledge, the absolute certainty that I have, I *have* seen this show before. I have.

I have, I have, I *have*.

But then maybe it's not just a show, not just a picture, some silly keepsake you'll plop on a bookshelf and forget until the next time you move and you need to make room for the newer, more important memories from your life.

It's a story.

A story like the one on that laminated paper.

Then it hits me. That's what this man—*Irving*, I say to myself, *Irving, though my friends call me Pretty Boy Number One*—is. He's a story. He wasn't giving me the hard sell or sinking the hook into my flesh; he was the hook.

I laugh to myself as I reach for my wallet again, sad to see I've only got a few dollars more, a fearful pang at the thought that maybe Irving won't give me the portrait after all since, really, what was the difference between a handful of dollars and a handful and a half? I brace myself for what might come next.

"Sorry, Irving. I—"

But already he's cackling again, grin bright and white as ever, hand held fast to my shoulder as he rocks and smiles and ooooh boys and oh, you somethin' else, Pretty Boys, all the while the pad just beyond my seeing.

"Oh, Pretty *Boy*! My sweet little *Number Two*. See now, with that much, I can get somebody a sandwich, maybe even two. See now, Pretty Boy—well, Pretty

Boy Number Two, I should say. I'm Pretty Boy Number One, right? Don't you forget it. Don't you forget that. But that's better, Pretty Boy. I can do somethin' with that. Can really help somebody with that. Make a difference. You character. You ham. You pretty, pretty *boy*."

The money's already gone; either I hadn't been paying close enough attention or there really was some ratty magic to the man because I look once and then I look again and it's gone and he's laughing and pointing and leaned back easy again, eyes bright as his teeth, the hardness gone now, touching up the portrait here, there, here again, turning the page like he's done, then thinking better of it when he notices some vital element still lacking. He looks at me, looks back at the page, lifts the pencil like he's going to make another mark, then stops.

Something in my chest squeezes.

And then Alley is there, finally there, though I don't know that I want her to be. I feel something I might call relief, but it's sadder than I would have thought. I bow up against it, confused by it, almost fearful of it, the chill of the station somehow even sharper than before.

I don't want him to go, I realize. I don't want the story to be over.

"Hey, you two."

I introduce her to Irving.

"Oh. Hi, Irving."

Cackling again, he reaches for her with his free hand. They shake and he dissolves into a fit of giggles more powerful than anything I'd seen before.

"Oh, my, my, my. I *told* you I was famous. Yep. Yes. The Most Famous Man in Philadelphia. That's me. That's me. Pretty Boy, you done good. She's pretty, too. Not as pretty as you, though!"

He explodes, ripping the finished portrait free of the pad as carelessly as if he were planning to toss it directly into one of the station's many trash bins. I almost shout at him to *be careful*, just managing to bite my tongue before it pops free and Alley smiles at me, disbelieving, says she's going to check the train times, says it's getting late. A few feet away, she stops, turning back to make sure I'm okay. I wave her on.

I turn to find a rolled piece of paper wrapped in a rubber band extended toward me.

"How long you two been together?"

I tell him, seemingly the funniest thing Irving has ever heard.

"Good, that's… *good.*"

Then he's serious again, gripped tight to me with a hand stronger and steadier than before, than I ever would have or could have thought possible.

"You do somethin' for me, Pretty Boy. Pretty Boy Number Two. You get home tonight and you take her hand, you take ya girl's hand and you look into her eyes and you tell her she's beautiful, okay? You tell her she's beautiful, and that you love her. Not because she's beautiful. Nothin' stupid like that. No, you tell her that because she's yours, okay? Because she's yours and you're hers. Because together, you two make a home. Together, you two are home. She's your home, Pretty Boy. You get it? You hear me, Pretty Boy? You get me?"

I nod, awash in a fresh burst of giggles.

"Oh, you character. You *ham.*"

He stands, stiff and slow, pushing himself away from the back of the bench with one long arm as he lets the length of metal just below his knee take the full weight of his body. He pushes the portrait into my hands.

"You remember what I said?"

I tell him I do.

He smiles and giggles and starts off, muttering to himself about me, about Pretty Boy, about Pretty Boy Number Two, such a character, such a *ham*, my eye seeming to slip involuntarily from the scarecrow stretch of his impossibly thin shoulders to the board where the times and tracks flip, updating once more.

I mean to watch him, to see where he goes next, who his next subject will be, but then I remember Alley and our train and the queue and I turn to see her waving, the hand she'd given to Irving motioning me toward Track 9. I'm next to her, explaining everything, trying to piece together what exactly had happened, when I remember Irving, when I remember wanting to follow him to his next stop. I search for him beyond the crowd collected at the top of the stairs, but it seems he's already gone.

But then maybe that was him shuffling over to the trashcan by Track 13, peering down into its depths like he was expecting to find some long-awaited treasure. Or maybe that was him looking out through the sectioned glass doors at the traffic on Market, bouncing so much his puffy down jacket seems to fall right off his shoulders. But no, that wasn't him. Those people weren't him, any more than

96

the woman with the stain on her sweatshirt and the winter hat pulled down so low it covered one of her eyes, the only good one she seemingly had left, was.

Already, I'm having trouble even remembering his face, those bright white teeth, his hard, determinedly happy eyes. I'm looking over the people around me and thinking, he could be anyone, he could be anywhere, even if he couldn't be anything, sorry, Irv, the world just ain't as welcoming as it used to be. Or, well, as welcoming as we all *wish* it used to be. How it could be.

But then I think, maybe he was still there. Maybe he was still there, somewhere, watching me, waiting. Or maybe looking for someone else. The next mark. The next *ham*. The next character to sketch, the next spirit to touch.

Maybe he was there. Maybe he'd always be there.

Maybe.

Maybe.

Maybe.

Made in the USA
Coppell, TX
15 October 2020